# Parklife Hideaways

COTTAGES AND CABINS IN
NORTH AMERICAN PARKLANDS

gestalten

PARKS PROJECT

# Parklife

## Lessons for Living in the Majestic Parklands

So much of the world we build for ourselves echoes the natural majesty of the environment around us. However, we are constantly at odds with nature when we create dwelling spaces, places for refuge, and shelter from the elements—forever balancing the rugged, organic wonder of the world surrounding us with our human love of comfort. In this way, we almost instinctively curate places that suit our need for comfort, reconciling with them *in situ* in our best attempts at merging the natural with the man-made.

It shouldn't come as a surprise that the homes that we find near parks often reflect and hold the wonder of the world outside. At the same time, they protect and shelter, allowing their tenants to explore and take in the miraculous views protected by our parklands in safety and comfort. One might struggle to think of anything more idyllic than firewood crackling in a hearth, while outside snow flurries onto the peaks of the Grand Tetons. Equally, one might be challenged to

conceive of anything more atmospheric than the steady drum of raindrops on the roof of an Airstream looking out at Half Dome in Yosemite, California, or the smell of sage and wet desert soil wafting through an open window to fill a rustic space with the scents of Canyonlands National Park.

Our parks are sanctuaries of wonder, and it doesn't take much to conclude that it is only natural—especially now, in the age of rampant technology—to seek them out for a reprieve from the mundane and over-saturated in favor of the wild. They provide an escape from the known and a portal to the unknown, a domain where humans can only be partners with nature and not masters of it. In this way, the cabins, shacks, and other dwellings we occupy as we explore parks are little more than outposts, home bases as we adventure into our personal unknowns. In this book, you will find a variety of inspiring homes with exploration and contemplation in mind, places whose designs are calibrated to merge with and celebrate their environments, with as little intervention into their fragile ecosystems as possible.

As we open doors to the wonders of these natural environments, we learn more about them—and ultimately, more about ourselves. They inspire us to think more deeply about our place in the world and the responsibility we have of being entrusted with its protection. Parks are invaluable communal spaces, open to people of all backgrounds, where individuals can come together to share meals, enjoy each other's company, and contribute significantly to the enriching tapestry of the human experience. They are also places where we remember history and the people who were the original stewards of these lands; preserving the culture of those who first dwelled here—and continue to do so today—is yet another reason why it is essential that parks remain protected.

In combination, these elements present us with an opportunity that has been my life's work to date—to leave these places better than we found them. Whether the door to your next adventure opens to islands off the coast of California, a soot-black canyon in western Colorado, or a painted sunset of reds, purples, and oranges in Maine, I hope the freedom of the parks inspires you to protect these wonderful, one-of-a-kind places and continue to explore the unparalleled beauty of North America's parklands.

Parks have the power to not only educate us but also change us for the better, and as their guardians and stewards, we have a duty to ensure that the lessons they impart do not end with us. So, find that perfect cabin in the woods, that beach-side shack, or hut hewn from stone, and give yourself the gift of freedom in places that have the power to change and inspire. I know firsthand the ability they have to change lives for the better.

*Parks Project is a certified B Corp lifestyle brand that designs best-in-market apparel, home goods, and outdoor accessories that inspire the exploration and conservation of parklands. The brand has given over $2.5 million back to parks since 2014 and is committed to donating at least a quarter of its profits to causes aligned with its mission to leave nature better than we found it.*

Keith Eshelman is the co-founder of Parks Project.

YOSEMITE NATIONAL PARK

# A Rustic Getaway in the Heart of the Hudson Valley Forest

TIVOLI BARN
TIVOLI, NEW YORK

On the banks of Stoney Creek, just two hours from New York City, Tivoli Barn feels a world away from city life. This unique retreat is nestled in the Hudson Valley, which is peppered with farms, hiking trails, and quaint towns with lively main streets. Just a few minutes' walk from the small village of Tivoli, this 1800s barn has been stylishly converted to welcome visitors in need of a retreat from the Big Apple.

The owners are intentional about maintaining the property's rustic charm, which also includes a picturesque and modern two-bedroom cottage. The barn's spacious two stories can accommodate up to six guests.

In the living area of the barn, wicker chairs adorned with sheepskins hang

elegantly from the ceiling, and a couch in the corner beckons for an afternoon read. The classic Vermont Castings woodstove adds to the cozy ambience. Windows look out on the surrounding forest with over twenty different species of mature trees whose beauty shifts and evolves throughout the seasons. The fully equipped chef's kitchen is ready for farm-to-table gourmet creations made from produce found at the local farmers' market. Upstairs, beds are tucked into two different sleeping nooks, separated by privacy curtains, with a separate loft bedroom above. Situated on 4 acres (1.6 hectares), the property takes full advantage of its remote wooded setting with multiple outdoor hangouts. The barn features a spacious black locust deck with an outdoor shower. A wooden platform is perched above the creek with a pebble beach close by. Paths lead through the woods and down to the pond where there is a picnic table, and a firepit circled by Adirondack chairs is tucked in a clearing among the trees.

This relaxing and calm setting is welcoming all year round—the sound of the wind in the trees or the rush of the stream becomes the soundtrack to a relaxing weekend far away from the stresses of city life.

TIVOLI BARN

TIVOLI BARN

# A Family's Forest Sanctuary Rooted in Rural Maine Tradition

PIERI PINES
OTISFIELD, MAINE

In Maine, the term "camp" is used to refer to small, rustic cabins and lakeside getaways, evoking the relaxed spirit of family weekends spent at a more casual pace away from the cares of everyday life. Tapping into this long-standing tradition and the ethos of simple, relaxed living, three brothers built the Pieri Pines sanctuary as a place to gather for family retreats. Carved by glaciers, this is a landscape of forest, water, and stones. Trees are the backbone of both the materials and the surrounding natural environment—Maine is after all known as the "Pine Tree State." The house's simple but elegant siding is crafted from locally sourced eastern white cedar, a nod to the forest that surrounds it and infuses the building with character.

The modern take on well-known materials embraces and honors the deep-seated traditions of Maine's camp vernacular and helps to make this space feel like it fits, glove-like, into its natural surroundings. With the landscape as both inspiration and creative constraint, the house took shape through sectional planning and is designed around a glacial boulder. The deck outside the living room hugs this massive geological formation, while the second floor seems to effortlessly hover above.

With focus placed on communal living and strengthening family bonds, the house is designed to bring the families together. To keep things balanced, all three bedrooms are equally sized so that none of them dominate as the primary space. Instead, it's the communal areas that reign and welcome everyone in, with a spacious family room and cozy window seating encircling an enormous kitchen table. In warmer weather, the communal space expands onto the deck, and with a short stroll down the slope, onto the lake dock. The perfect retreat for family summer getaways that encourages a deep sense of connection.

# A Tiny Treetop Cabin Close to the Remote Catskill Mountains

HALF-TREE HOUSE:
BEAVER BROOK
SULLIVAN COUNTY,
NEW YORK

On a remote piece of land near the Catskills, nature is the ultimate creative collaborator. With no vehicle access, no piped water, no electricity, and an incredibly arduous topography, the challenges of this 60-acre (24-hectare) location were just one aspect of a demanding design. The other? It being constructed on a limited budget and entirely by its two owners, along with a little help from their friends.

Situated on a steep slope, the physical demands of the site became the structure's signature detail. Using surrounding trees as a structural element—the timber framing anchored with bolts commonly found in treehouses—eliminated the need for large footings, retaining walls, and pumped con-

crete, and initial sitework was done by hand with shovels. The result is a 360-square-foot (33 square-meter) cabin cantilevered over the hillside, seemingly floating above the ground, as if hanging among the tree branches.

Both the interior and exterior use boards made from Eastern pines, sourced locally from the property, all milled and kiln dried. The outside is treated with traditional Scandinavian pine tar, helping to minimize maintenance during long wet winters, and adding a distinct black and modern aesthetic that blends the building into the forest. The structure is painted white inside, accentuating the light and adding a sense of spaciousness to an otherwise cozy single room.

A creative exercise in minimalism, the space is outfitted with only essential necessities, including an efficient Jøtul woodstove. When it's needed, power comes from a portable generator.

Trees are not just a structural component of this creative space. The enormous steel-tube pivot doors fitted with dual-insulated glass that span from floor to ceiling, make the forest something that you don't just look at but that you are a part of. It might be called a "half-tree house" but within its cozy interior, you're fully enveloped in your own little treetop nest.

24                                    HALF-TREE HOUSE: BEAVER BROOK

# A Tranquil Family Base Camp on Oregon's Rugged Coast

THE CAPE
CAPE MEARES, OREGON

When a young couple stumbled upon this 1990s house on the Oregon Coast, they immediately fell in love. Despite the mildewy bathroom and weathered condition from harsh coastal wind and rain, the potential was clear. Inspired by their background in mountaineering and guiding, the owners set out to turn the place into an extended base camp for their family—a place to enjoy the environment, revel in coastal exploration, converse over meals and games, and spend quality time together.

The 1,200-square-foot (111-square-meter) house is spread out over three levels. The ground level includes a mudroom, bathroom, and bedroom, but the focal point of the space is on the second floor, which houses the living

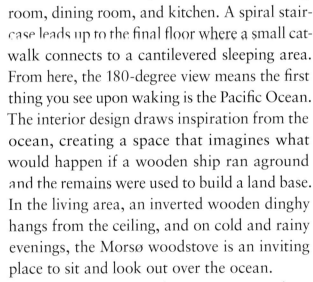

room, dining room, and kitchen. A spiral staircase leads up to the final floor where a small catwalk connects to a cantilevered sleeping area. From here, the 180-degree view means the first thing you see upon waking is the Pacific Ocean. The interior design draws inspiration from the ocean, creating a space that imagines what would happen if a wooden ship ran aground and the remains were used to build a land base. In the living area, an inverted wooden dinghy hangs from the ceiling, and on cold and rainy evenings, the Morsø woodstove is an inviting place to sit and look out over the ocean.

Much of the design and renovation was done by the owners themselves, and reclaimed materials were used whenever possible, with wood sourced from century-old homes in Portland, and a slab of yellow pine from a bowling alley that makes up the dining table.

With its faded cedar shingling, the house evolves with its environment, and the owners wanted the same for the area surrounding the building. Removing the sparse lawn, they replanted the area with native marsh and dune grasses, adding in shore pines, black pines, dwarf pines, and sword ferns, making the entire space fit seamlessly into the coastal landscape.

THE CAPE

# A Western Washington Retreat Overlooking the Bay of Port Susan

KAYAK POINT HOUSE
PORT SUSAN, WASHINGTON

Nestled atop the mainland's precipice in Western Washington, the Kayak Point House gazes through the evergreen foliage towards the water and islands beneath it. With the Cascade Range to the east, and the Olympics to the west, the architecture of this intimate home begins with the statuesque cedar trees that rise into the Pacific Northwest sky. These giants have long been considered the "tree of life" by Indigenous Coast Salish people, and they create the cornerstones of this intimate home—the blueprint for a house that's intentionally designed to have a strong connection to place. The house is nestled among the trees, and in the living room, the floor-to-ceiling windows face west towards Camano Island, with evergreens framing the view. Peek through to look out at the saltwater, glittering on sunny days and moodier on gray ones, often accented by the glorious pinks and oranges at sunset. The strong sense of place that is the backbone of the design is replicated elsewhere in the house. Sliding sunroom doors make for a seamless transition between indoor and outdoor spaces on warmer days. Forever in reverence to the natural world that surrounds it, the guest room has windows that look directly out on one of the enormous cedar trunks.

In a relatively small space, sliding walls provide more flexibility in how the space is used. Throughout the house, there are areas for either intimate nestling or luxurious outspreading. By the woodstove, the exposed beams and rafters sit high above, creating a palatial and elevated feel. In other parts of the house, ceilings are low enough that you can almost touch them, instilling a sense of coziness. This layering of spaces and carefully considered sight lines creates movement and interest, pulling you through the house and offering up an interior sense of depth, reinforced by the vast trees and landscape.

KAYAK POINT HOUSE

KAYAK POINT HOUSE

# Building in Harmony with Nature

The founding principles of America's parkitecture remain the backbone of wilderness building styles today.

The terrain in the immediate vicinity of Yellowstone's Old Faithful, arguably the most famous geological attraction in America's most iconic national park, is predominantly characterized by hills cloaked in pine trees. When it isn't projecting 200°F (93°C) water nearly as many feet into the air, the famous geyser remains invisible. What's left to the eye of any visitor surveying the scene is the basin's built landscape, and chief among the buildings there is the Old Faithful Inn.

Flanked by two wings extending nearly 700 feet (213 meters) in total length, the inn's striking central structure features a steeply pitched roof that rises nearly 100 feet (30 meters) into the sky, adorned with multiple levels of dormers and topped with flags. If it were made of steel and concrete, the building might impose on those hills, but its architect, Robert Reamer, limited the inn's design to the local materials available at the time of its construction between 1903 and 1904: lodgepole pine and rhyolite stone. The effect is that looking at the Old Faithful Inn is much like looking at a very large log cabin—at a building that, despite being the grandest in a landscape that's mostly building-free, appears to be exactly where it ought to be.

That everlasting sense of belonging is why many consider the Old Faithful Inn among the best examples of "parkitecture," the architectural style more formally known as National Park Service Rustic, which emerged during the first decades of the 20th century as the United States began setting aside the country's most resplendent areas of natural beauty for protection and recreation.

Until the U.S. National Park Service (NPS) was founded in 1916, development in the existing parks was largely left up to concessioners (mostly railroad companies) and the U.S. Army. The NPS aimed for a more thoughtful, guided approach, and prioritized a feeling of belonging in taking on the task of park development. Its first policy statement, written in 1918, avowed that "In the construction of roads, trails, buildings, and other improvements, particular attention must be devoted

*This page:* The Old Faithful Inn at Yellowstone National Park. *Opposite:* Richard L. Proenneke's hand-built log cabin at Upper Twin Lake in Alaska. *Page 42:* The Paradise Inn at Mount Rainier National Park.

always to the harmonizing of these improvements with the landscape."

The current park buildings had incorporated various architectural styles, including Victorian, Colonial Revival, and Neoclassical elements. The most successful were those that leaned on approaches stemming from the Arts and Crafts movement and took nature as inspiration; notably, Adirondack style, which drew from Swiss chalets but used native and often irregular materials, and Frank Lloyd Wright's grounded horizontal Prairie style. The cultural past also played a role—pioneer cabins, Spanish adobe structures, and Native American dwellings, with all their encapsulated nostalgia for prior wilderness settlers, were also deemed appropriate influences for future park buildings.

One early success was the Grand Canyon's Hopi House, designed by Mary Colter and constructed in 1905. Colter envisioned the building in the Pueblo style with stone masonry, sandstone walls, and thatched ceilings supported by log beams to resemble authentic Hopi architecture. Another triumph was its neighbor, the El Tovar Hotel, even though that building has an entirely different design based on local limestone and pine timber. Fitting in need not take one form.

Hotels in particular—the great hotels, as they're known—were the early showpieces of the national parks. To get the public to the newly protected wilderness, officials and architects had to create places to stay—these would receive fitting attention, both inside and outside. Mount Rainier's Paradise Inn might look like other grand gabled lodges (if a little bunker-like to withstand the mountain's blizzards) but it's lobby is a uniquely vast realm of log beams and massive stone fireplaces inhabited by original rustic cedar tables and seating, and parchment lantern-like lights above decorated with local plant life. Glacier Park Lodge's great hall is an even more impressive vault held up by towering Douglas firs with their bark left as intact as it is in the forests beyond its walls. The national park does not end at the threshold where the hotel begins; the park enters through the door.

The variability and maturation of park style found a high point in Yosemite's Ahwahnee Hotel, built between 1925 and 1927. Its lead architect, Gilbert Stanley Underwood, had trained within the Arts and Crafts tradition and had already wielded that education in desert-themed lodges in Zion and Bryce Canyon. But in the Ahwahnee, he produced a truly distinct building that reflected the unique setting of Yosemite while still employing the materials and motifs found in other parks—logs for the interior support, and natural stone pillars outside that draw the eye upward toward the valley's granite walls. Rather than rustic, the inside is filled with more modern wood furnishings and plenty of Native American art motifs—in the lobby's floor mosaics, running along the cornices, within the Great Lounge's iconic stained-glass windows, and beyond. Like the other park hotels of the era, the Ahwahnee is grand but not so much that it draws attention away from Yosemite Falls or Half Dome. As one historian once put it, "It seemed almost small."

The parks also needed ranger stations, interpretive museums, maintenance buildings, picnic areas, lookout towers, and entrance gates. The NPS's notions of rustic style had been interpreted largely by its leaders on a

The Ahwahnee Hotel in Yosemite, California, built in the 1920s, featured then-modern wood furnishings and Native Amerian motifs.

case-by-case basis. This was observed first-hand by Thomas Vint who, throughout the 1920s and early '30s, ascended from the rank of draftsman working with Underwood and another prominent park architect named Herbert Maier to chief of the Branch of Plans and Designs (helping create Glacier's Going-to-the-Sun Road, one of the most famous scenic drives in North America).

One of Vint's missions at the NPS was to standardize things. At the end of the 1920s, he was pivotal in creating a master plan program for long-term park development, which came in handy in 1933 when the resources of the Civilian Conservation Corps (CCC) and Public Works Administration (PWA) were put at the parks' disposal. This infusion of manpower, however, made it impossible for Vint and other leaders to attend to each individual project; seemingly all at once, parkitecture needed codification. Vint's team supplied it, as noted by Albert Good in *Park Structures and Facilities,* a textbook published in 1935 by the Division of Planning to help train the CCC forces. Good writes that NPS Rustic "is a style which, through the use of native materials in proper scale, and through the avoidance of severely straight lines and over-sophistication, gives the feeling of having been executed by pioneer craftsmen with limited hand tools. It thus achieves sympathy with natural surroundings and with the past."

Despite this formal manual, that same infusion of resources came accompanied by new ideas about architecture—the simpler forms of modernism played nicely with new building

*Bottom left:* Parkitecture-inspired interiors at Blackberry Farm in the Great Smoky Mountains; *top right:* Kapalaoa Cabin in Hawaii's Haleakalā National Park.

materials and techniques that were easier to execute, repeat, and maintain. Modernism looked forward, not back, and this reaction against pioneer romanticism went hand in hand with World War II budgetary requirements and a growing need for faster park development to push the rustic style out its log-framed door.

But even if the formal rustic style fell out of favor, its individual principles remain a trove of oft-employed ideas on how to create buildings that exist in harmony with their surroundings. The idea that buildings set in areas of significant natural beauty should blend in remains strong—not only within the civic bounds of the parklands but also in all the wild reaches where humans resolve to establish dwellings.

No building embodies the spirit and aims of parkitecture quite like a cabin. Cabins were built across national and state parks, often in similar and sometimes precisely repeated designs, because they so easily meshed with the wilderness landscape. "So accustomed are we to survivals of frontier cabins dotting the countryside," writes Good, "that we have grown to look upon them as almost indigenous to a natural setting." Cabins exist in our collective imagination of wilderness just as mountains, rivers, forests, and deserts do.

This might explain why Richard "Dick" Proenneke chose to retire in 1968 to the remote

Alaskan wilderness near Twin Lakes, which later became Lake Clark National Park and Preserve in 1980. There, he constructed a log cabin entirely by hand, using traditional tools and techniques. And perhaps that's also why Proenneke had the foresight to film the entire construction process, why so many watched that footage when it was released as a documentary, and why so many make the pilgrimage to see the cabin for themselves.

Cabins do not necessarily need to be constructed from logs, nor do they have to be located in isolated wilderness areas. They represent efficiency and self-sufficiency in a world where such qualities are more and more rare. It's no wonder that they served as inspiration for the back-to-the-land movement of the '60s and '70s, or that cabins feature

*This page:* Zion Park Lodge in Utah's Zion National Park.
*Opposite:* A Lake Tahoe retreat that brings the outdoors in.

"A straight line can be drawn from Lloyd Kahn's ideas through the decades to contemporary cabins and wilderness structures."

heavily in the works of Lloyd Kahn, one of that movement's most notable advocates. Just as parkitecture looked to early pioneer cabins for inspiration, Kahn, in his 1973 opus-slash-building manual, *Shelter,* looked to the huts of the Maasai and Kabye, to Bedouin tents, to the yurts of Central Asia, the dwellings of North America's Indigenous people, and beyond for ways to live closer to nature and with less impact. Kahn's ideas have and continue to draw and inspire countless others. His foundational principles for what makes a successful building? Use local materials, and make it look like it's part of its surroundings. Thomas Vint would surely have approved.

A straight line can be drawn from Kahn's ideas through the decades to contemporary cabins and wilderness structures. For many

of these buildings, it's not enough to blend in with nature, they seek to bring the outside in—with massive windows, skylights, sliding doors, and spacious decks that blur the line between indoor and outdoor living spaces. Some seek to blend in with natural exteriors or dark finishes while others are so sleek that they make their presence known, like the Ahwahnee does. Even those that lack a trace of their rustic antecedents outside are bound to contain elements of the cultural past: vintage furniture and decor ranging from pre-rustic to mid-century modern. And in these spaces, a prominently placed woodstove is all but guaranteed, allowing dwellings of any size to have a great hall of their own.

Modern cabins may not be made of hand-hewn rock and timber sourced from the same land they sit upon—though some are—and they might not subjugate themselves to their surroundings. But even with contemporary materials and plenty of straight lines, the best of them still do what the architects, designers, and planners of the national parks hoped their hotels and ranger stations and visitor centers would: they fit in, and they create a sense of place.

# An Off-Grid Lake Retreat Tucked in the Adirondack Mountains

REMOTE LAKE CABIN
MOUNTAIN LAKE,
NEW YORK

At the edge of a lake in the Adirondacks sits this off-grid cabin, built to sit lightly on the land. The family who built the retreat has a special affinity and connection to the area with roots dating back five generations, so building in a way that respected the local landscape was paramount. No road access meant that everything, including materials and machinery, had to be floated in by small boat or raft.

Every effort was made to reduce impact and keep the site as pristine as possible. Set in the heart of a densely wooded forest, the cabin was designed to minimize the number of trees to be felled, and those that were cut were saved to be used in the woodstove. Conventional machinery was

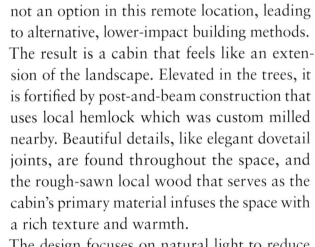

not an option in this remote location, leading to alternative, lower-impact building methods. The result is a cabin that feels like an extension of the landscape. Elevated in the trees, it is fortified by post-and-beam construction that uses local hemlock which was custom milled nearby. Beautiful details, like elegant dovetail joints, are found throughout the space, and the rough-sawn local wood that serves as the cabin's primary material infuses the space with a rich texture and warmth.

The design focuses on natural light to reduce the need for electricity, but when needed, power is provided by a remote solar field. As the night gets darker, candles flicker in the kitchen. The main living space extends outside onto the deck through a large glass window and door, and in the bathroom, the windows open straight into the forest.

The modest 780-square-foot (72-square-meter) cabin houses five people, and sustainability was taken into consideration at every turn with zero-low VOC finishes, wood heat, natural light, and passive solar design. These sustainable touches are yet another sign of respect for the land and make for a beautiful space that considers the well-being of its inhabitants.

REMOTE LAKE CABIN

# A Creative Retreat Where Nature is the Muse

OFFSITE CAMP—CABIN 01
WASSAIC, NEW YORK

We all crave a retreat from everyday life, but a refuge can also exist to fuel a creative work practice. That's what this cabin is for, designed as a space for remote work, and envisioned as a prototype for a new way of immersing oneself in the outdoors to inspire and encourage creativity. Just a couple of hours' train ride or drive away from New York City, it's an ideal escape for creative city dwellers that need some restorative time. At only 225 square feet (21 square meters), the space is humble but asks the visitor to consider the endless options that its location might inspire. Built on a trailer, the cabin is intended to be easily transportable. At the time of writing, the cabin is perched atop a clearing in the mountains outside

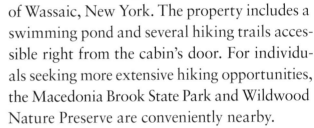

of Wassaic, New York. The property includes a swimming pond and several hiking trails accessible right from the cabin's door. For individuals seeking more extensive hiking opportunities, the Macedonia Brook State Park and Wildwood Nature Preserve are conveniently nearby.

Water holding tanks, solar power with a propane generator backup system, and a composting toilet make the building entirely off-grid. However, creatives that need to stay connected can do so via satellite internet service.

The cabin exudes a warm yet minimalist ambiance, with just enough flourishes to keep the creative drive going. Warm wood is contrasted with dark green tiles in the bathroom, and the built-in storage that separates the bed and desk has a small library of curated books on wellness and outdoor living. The wooden deck features Adirondack chairs and a firepit, or for those who want a bigger blaze, there is plenty of firewood on hand for bonfires.

The design may be modern, but the creative ethos is nothing new as the area has a long history of being home to artists. From its unique perspective overlooking the expansive valley below, nature is the ultimate creative muse in this cozy off-grid cabin.

OFFSITE CAMP—CABIN 01

# Rustic Elegance Meets Sustainability in This Hudson Valley Hideaway

FOX HALL HOUSE
COLUMBIA COUNTY,
NEW YORK

On a drive through New York's bucolic Hudson Valley, it's not unusual to see an old barn overlooking a thatch of farmland or a cluster of historic buildings peeking through the trees. That's why Fox Hall House, a forested compound comprising a 2,100-square-foot (195-square-meter) home, a 19th-century barn, and a garage, might not warrant a glance. And yet, each aspect of Fox Hall House, from its custom millwork to Vermont-sourced-wood roof supports, surprises upon closer inspection. For owner Ian Hague and architecture and design firm BarlisWedlick, sustainability was the guiding principle of the project. Set on a 75-acre (30-hectare) parcel protected by the Columbia Land Conservancy, both

the main home and the 180-year-old barn (relocated from a nearby farm) were designed using *passive house* standards which aim to create homes and buildings that consume very little energy while also achieving a high level of comfort and quality.

The regal and impressive barn houses entertaining spaces and a bedroom and showcases a wooden exterior burnt to an inky hue using the Shou Sugi Ban technique—plus thick walls for superior insulation. The roof supports include a built-in photovoltaic array to supply power. Triple-paned windows, most notably two walls of glass that come together in the living room, maximize solar gain and connection to the landscape. Freestanding millwork shells create "rooms" while allowing for the barn's natural open flow.

Outdoors, delicate bridges connect buildings. A sauna anchors a three-story, treehouse-like tower; a screened-in porch crowns the top, skirting the highest branches. And then there is the swimming pool, chlorine-free, and filtered by plants.

Many vintage furnishings and locally commissioned pieces, alongside Hague's global collection, adorn the space.

61

FOX HALL HOUSE

FOX HALL HOUSE

# Off-Grid Minimalism in Alaska's Chugach National Forest

CORK CABIN 1+2
MOOSE PASS, ALASKA

Off-the-grid in the heart of the Kenai Peninsula, a compound made of two cork-clad cabins is nestled into a hill at the base of the surrounding rugged mountains. From afar, the silhouettes seem to be meticulously cut, simple geometric shapes that softly declare their presence.

A small footpath leads from the parking lot to the deck, with a cabin on either side, perfectly framing the vista between the two mountain peaks that rise up beyond the lake below. Between them, a sunken firepit, made from equally angular geometry, beckons for an evening blaze. If you're lucky, on darker nights it is possible to watch the sky get painted with the colors of the aurora borealis.

Open the solid timber door to the smaller 250-square-foot (23-square-meter) cabin and step into its cedar-scented interior, infused with the fragrance of the forest. Made from prefabricated dowel-laminated timber panels, the interior is exactly the same as the outside. The thermal mass of this timber construction helps to hold heat for longer, making it an energy-efficient build for the Alaskan climate.

The smaller cabin houses a modest cooking and dining space as well as sleeping platforms. The larger 750-square-foot (70-square-meter) cabin is designed for longer-term living functionality. Upstairs there are additional sleeping spaces, and the interior is clad with whitewashed oak veneer plywood. Matched with the oak hardwood floors, the result is a calming interior.

Entirely off-grid, the larger cabin has an array of solar panels positioned on the tilted facade of the second floor, blending into the structure. Underneath the cabin, a 1,100-gallon (4,164-liter) tank collects rainwater.

The outer cork that clads the facades is used as an insulation layer. In the warmer months, the warm cork exterior is offset by the lush, bright-green hillsides, and in winter, by a subtler contrast of white snow-covered landscape.

CORK CABIN 1+2

# A Clifftop Cabin Nestled in the Vast Wilderness of Eastern Canada

Entwined in the forest's shifting splendor, this off-grid hideaway reflects the spirit of its owner and the natural world that envelopes it.

"No house should ever be on a hill. It should be of the hill, belonging to it," said architect Frank Lloyd Wright. Three years after sketching a plan on the back of a pizza box, Sacha Roy, the owner of this cliffside cabin—nestled in a forest of yellow birch, oak, hemlock, and sugar maple—has artfully fulfilled that vision with a home that mirrors the natural world enveloping it. Built entirely from scratch, the cabin needed only five trees to make way for its modest footprint, and all cues were taken from the local landscape: the exterior stairs, as well as the wraparound deck and gardens which follow the shape of the cliff and provide expansive views over networks of branches, surrounding mountains, and the glinting river below. Inside, the red pine is raw and unpainted, its creaking and sighing conjuring the sensation of being safely ensconced in an ancient tree.

With 20-foot (6-meter) ceilings, the cabin feels uncluttered, airy, and deeply entwined with the forest's shifting moods: "Facing south and high up on the cliff, you can't help but wake up with the first light," says Roy of the cozy loft bedroom. "You can smell the cedar, the pine, the fresh air making its way along the cliff, and the soil of the forest. You can sense the changing seasons, hear trees drop seeds to the forest floor, and birds that let you witness the timeline of migration...This home has given me an attentiveness to what's happening all around me."

The choice of this profoundly peaceful setting in Eastern Canada grew out of a yearning to plant some roots after years traveling the globe as a documentary filmmaker. "I wanted to find a space to feel free from unnecessary stress," says Roy. "I've always been more creative in a vast space." Drawing on memories of childhood vacations at a rustic cottage and the picturesque yet hardy fishermen's cabins that dot the coast of Nova Scotia, he began to envision a quiet refuge from city life. At first, he camped out on the patch of land where the cabin is currently set, battling mosquitoes and "shaking hands with the place," before plunging into the challenges of building. Before construction could begin, it was necessary to build a trail and elevator to haul material up from the bottom of the cliff. A friend helped lay the foundations, anchoring concrete pads into the granite rock, while a professional framer assisted with the shell of the home. From there, Roy plugged on alone between film jobs. "It was the beginning of a new adventure, and I wanted it to be personal," he says, determined to outsource as little as possible, and guided by the belief that anything he crafted by himself, he'd be able to fix by himself too.

When the ambitious project began, Roy didn't own a single tool; one mammoth learning curve and roughly $130,000 later, the filmmaker became an authority on the highs and lows of off-grid living, providing hard-earned advice and even blueprints to aspiring self-starters. (He posts as Canadian Castaway on Instagram.) Today, his remote cabin is entirely self-sufficient, with a rainwater tank, septic system, drinking water from a UV system, and a glowing woodstove that sits in the heart of the space. Solar power allows him to run a fridge, a small washing machine, and even a video-editing studio with internet (as long as he's mindful of cloudy days). It doesn't mean a life entirely independent of fossil fuels though—yet. "But it does set us up to visualize exactly how much energy we use, and why, so we can consider ways to move into a new realm without them," says Roy. That's an ongoing journey of fine-tuning—from the charming but impractical feed-trough bathtub that had to be upgraded to the leaky salvaged windows that might one day require the same. "It will never truly be finished," he says of his beguiling hideout among the trees. "It's continually evolving and adapting to changing needs and seasons."

"You can smell the cedar, the pine, the fresh air making its way along the cliff, and the soil of the forest. You can sense the changing seasons."

SACHA ROY/CANADIAN CASTAWAY

# A Cozy Shelter in the Heart of a Southwestern Québec Park

LE PIC
LAURENTIDES, QUÉBEC

The Poisson Blanc Reservoir in Southwestern Québec is dotted with islands, and the regional park is known for its idyllic wild campsites at the water's edge. For those who want a little more comfort, the park worked with Atelier L'Abri to capture that same spirit in a micro-shelter.

Tucked into the trees at the end of a wooded path, this tiny cabin is only accessible by foot. You'll need snowshoes or skis in frigid Québec winters. As you approach from the park's reception area, the single-pitched roof rises up, covering a balcony that juts out and faces the forest and lake. Clad in native cedar, the exterior siding will eventually be grayed by time, which will slowly blend it into the natural surroundings.

From the outside, Le Pic presents as one elongated unit, but step inside to find two seamless parts: the interior living space and the covered balcony that allows a connection to the outdoors even when the elements don't cooperate. On warmer summer evenings, you can climb the ladder to the bed on the mezzanine.

A sliding glass door connects inner and outer areas, and leads from the covered balcony directly into the main living room and kitchen. Everything in this small space is meant to be multipurpose, with built-in furniture serving as storage, the kitchen, and seating. With ample natural light accented by the interior's soft timber paneling, the dining area looks out through the large bay window towards the serene view. Facing west, Le Pic affords private viewings of spectacular sunsets.

Built with durable and locally sourced materials, the unit is outfitted with solar LED lighting. The minimal yet efficient interior sleeps four to six people and has been optimized for storage and function. Firewood is stashed under the daybed and in the upstairs sleeping area, two custom-made double beds feature built-in storage and lighting. A perfectly placed window makes your waking view the forest outside.

MOUNT-TREMBLANT NATIONAL PARK

# A Secluded Backcountry Home in the Sierra Nevada Mountains

How an ex-pro athlete built a snowboarding Shangri-La on a slab of granite in California's High Sierra.

"Right now, I'm watching the sky change color from blue to orange to green while I cook dinner over the fire," says Mike Basich, describing his idyllic winter home 7,100 feet (2,164 meters) up Donner Summit, California. The pioneer snowboarding champion who established his roots in the punk days of the late-'80s shred scene and once dropped a mind-boggling 120 feet (37 meters) from a helicopter onto an Alaskan mountain, is now a photographer and off-grid nomad, having renounced a sprawling mansion in Utah for simpler, stripped-back living. Not only can the maverick snow-chaser roam wherever the mood and weather take him, courtesy of a tiny portable cabin hauled by his Dodge truck, but he also has his own powder paradise, perched on a slab of granite in the Sierra Nevada. Area-241, as Basich named his backcountry home (the moniker of his outerwear clothing label is Two For One), is his personal playground—accessible only by snowcat much of the year and equipped with its own chairlift. It's a diminutive house with the same idiosyncratic, easygoing charm of its owner: just one room, made from local stone with a curving design based on the golden ratio—a special number that can be found everywhere in nature, from plants and animals to star systems. Inside, a floor-inlaid pentagram radiates out to floor-to-ceiling windows that frame the pristine mountain scenery. The stove, couches, and shelves are built into the walls below a cozy loft bed. Out front, there's a wood-fired hot tub and cold plunge bath; since there's no indoor plumbing, a composting toilet sits outside too. Water comes from a nearby creek and electricity from solar panels. In an effort to preserve energy, Basich adheres to a routine of waking up with the first light of day as the sun rises and retiring for rest as night descends upon the landscape.

The stones laid into the path leading up to the 200-square-foot (18-square-meter) property are evidence of the grueling five-year build—they're carved with messages of goodwill from everyone who chipped in to help. Basich first lived in a teepee on his 40 acres (16 hectares) before beginning construction, to get a feel for weather patterns and the area's distinct personality. "I figured it out as I went," he says. "If I had shown up and started building right away, I would have been out of sync with the land. I wanted to build on the hilltop for the view, but also the wind helps me keep the snow off the roof. The sun keeps me warm with my large south-facing windows, meaning I need less firewood and storage space. I realized the best thing you can do is listen to nature. Up here, nature always wins." To say Area-241 is off the beaten track is an understatement—it's five miles to the local grocery store and ten from the storied railroad town of Truckee. "No one's showing up with a delivery truck out here, so every-

thing took much longer," he says. "I had to hand-mix cement myself, gather water, and move 175 tons (159 tonnes) of rock by hand." Still, the payback is priceless. "I get to see the stars without smog," he says. "I've learned so much about how we move with the sun. Building off-grid has given me gratitude wherever I go now—it's not often someone stays at your house and thanks you for having hot water. Living here has made me realize how out of balance we are with the Earth." From his vertiginous vantage point, Basich can see a storm rolling in miles away, alerting him to imminent snowfall and another chance to snowboard directly from his front door. If that sounds tempting, Basich has some advice for anyone looking to build their own off-grid aerie: "Don't think too hard," he says. "I see people all the time overthinking whether they can do it or not. I fail every day. It's the best way to learn. And tomorrow's a new day."

"I figured it out as I went. If I had shown up and started building right away, I would have been out of sync with the land."

MIKE BASICH/OFF-THE-GRID TAHOE CABIN

SIERRA NEVADA MOUNTAINS

# A Mountain Refuge for Nesting in the Columbia Valley Treetops

BIRD HUT
WINDERMERE,
BRITISH COLUMBIA

It might seem impossible that humans and birds—plus a flying squirrel or two—can cohabit in a single space. But that's exactly what happens at a snug perch in the woods of the Columbia Valley.

Architectural designer Mark Erickson of Studio North has been coming to his family's cabin in the area since he was a child. He describes the drive from Calgary as a majestic journey where each mile brings him closer to untouched nature. In 2018, it was these memories and his love of birds that inspired him to build the 100-square-foot (9-square-meter) Bird Hut—primarily used as a two-person bedroom—on the land near the family cabin. The hut, not unlike a bird's nest, rises high into the tree canopy. Lodgepole

pines salvaged from a forest fire are cross braced to suspend the hut 9 feet (3 meters) above the ground and a bridge connects it to the hillside. The poles cradle a platform made from reclaimed deck planks, and the little hut rests on the platform. Because the stilts cross in the center at one point load, they create a dynamic structure of movement, a slight sway to everything—precarious but in a pleasing way.

Inside, the hut houses a cozy bed with a leafy view through the polycarbonate ceiling. Similar to a greenhouse, the translucent roof also provides a source of passive solar heat ventilated by windows at the hut's entry and on its facade. The facade is where things get whimsical. It's here that Erickson incorporated species-specific birdhouses into the hut's exterior—twelve bird boxes in total, some small and low to the ground for chickadees and others bigger and higher up for woodpeckers. Winged creatures flit in and out of the boxes day and night to feed, chirp, socialize, and, of course, nest. The hut doesn't have electricity. The only illumination comes from the twinkling bulbs of string lights draped through tree branches. When seen from the communal firepit across the bridge, the overall effect is of nature at play.

# A Sanctuary at the Rocky Edge of Lake Superior

TRUE NORTH CABIN
EAGLE HARBOR, MICHIGAN

When the owners discovered this cabin perched above Lake Superior, they knew it would make the perfect base camp for exploring the surrounding wilderness. They had spent some time in the Pacific Northwest but returned to Keweenaw in Michigan's Upper Peninsula because of its solitude, unspoiled wilderness, and abundant wildlife. With Isle Royale National Park just to the north and plenty of opportunities to hike, fish, pedal, or paddle, the cabin is ideal for outdoor adventures or nature lovers looking to unwind. The cabin was designed by a Portland-based architect in the 1960s. Built with lumber shipped in from the Pacific Northwest, the cabin had a classic '60s look with orange countertops and brown appliances. Used only as an

occasional getaway, the cabin changed hands in 2018, and the new owners decided to remodel it for use as a vacation rental.

Instead of completely overhauling it, they honored the character and details of the original cabin, making modern refreshes. The orange countertops went, but much of the original wood cabinetry stayed intact. With two beds and one bath, the cabin sleeps up to four people and boasts an enormous indoor stone fireplace.

The glass railings of the wraparound deck make the cabin feel like it's part of the impressive Lake Superior landscape. Situated on a stretch of shoreline, it allows you to walk down steps from the deck and be directly on the lichen-covered rocky ledges where land meets lake. Even from the inside areas, the sunsets are stunning, and the nearby Keweenaw Dark Sky Park ensures incredible nighttime stargazing and even glimpses of the northern lights.

With no Wi-Fi or cell service, entertainment is provided by the local bald eagles, deer, loons, squirrels, and coyotes that roam the land. Close to beautiful wooded trails and waterfalls, the cabin makes for the perfect base camp, and while it's on a peninsula, you might just feel like you're tucked away on a secluded island instead.

# A Cozy Forest Escape Tucked in Québec's Gatineau Hills

DIY TINY A-FRAME
LOW, QUÉBEC

While many getaways and second homes are born of enormous budgets, a countryside escape does not have to be an extravagant affair. Andrew Szeto has inspired many with his tiny, low-budget A-frame project.

After finding a plot of land in the woods of Québec about an hour from his home, the woodworker and furniture maker with a love for the outdoors and adventure set out to design and build his own creation. Having honed his craft at the Ottawa City Woodshop, Szeto undertook the A-frame as his first project, and it was constructed simply on a tight budget. The work was done mainly by two people and an assortment of friends who offered to lend a hand.

Designed on a 10-by-10-foot (3-by-3-meter) base, the structure is intended as a landing pad for spending time outside and for enjoying relaxing weekends. Szeto reclaimed the doors and all but one window. A barrel structure that was originally built as an outhouse now serves as a sauna clad in siding made of wooden disks hewn from local branches.

The A-frame is just a five-minute walk from Lac George in Québec's Outaouais region and offers an easy launch for canoeing adventures, whether it's on a glorious summer day or a foggier fall afternoon. The local forest offers ample mushroom foraging opportunities, and winter affords snowier excursions.

The sloping metal roof is well suited to Québec winters, and its green shade helps it to blend into the surrounding forest. Inside there's a cozy living space that includes a couch and indoor climbing wall that doubles as access to the reading loft above. Four friends can sleep snugly indoors, but its small footprint also encourages outdoor living, cooking meals outside, and spending evenings warming by a bonfire. On colder days, you can cozy up inside where the wood stove will be cranking, creating the snuggest of weekend escapes.

DIY TINY A-FRAME

# A Lakeside A–Frame Renovation in the Evergreen Forest of Québec

CHALET A
MONTREAL, QUÉBEC

Situated in the Eastern Townships in Southeastern Québec, harsh Canadian winters make this lakefront cabin inaccessible for an entire season. Decades of those difficult conditions and neglect had taken their toll on this classic 1950s A-frame, but its recent revival has brought it into the 21st century with a beach cabin flair.

To get there is not for the faint of heart. A cascade of 150 steps leads down a steep hill to the cabin, which sits right on the edge of a pristine lake. The difficulty in accessing the A-frame made modern renovation a challenge, encouraging a flourish of creativity and ecological sensibility. Recovering as many existing materials as possible for the building process, the planners also added indigenous plants to the shoreline to help revitalize the lakefront.

Tucked into the evergreen forest, the cabin features playful interior spaces. Bookworms can suspend themselves above the living room in a reading net, and a separate dormitory pavilion adjacent to the main cabin helps to accommodate more guests. The building's centerpiece and muse is first and foremost the lake, and all details have this focal point in mind. Moving the A-frame main window inward accommodated a larger exterior dining area, perfect for lakeside dinners and listening to the waves. What was once cluttered and neglected now boasts a pared-back and fresh aesthetic that's intended to instill a sense of calm while also keeping the attention on the outdoor surroundings. Fresh white and sage tones brighten the space, while white pine flooring, exposed timber framing, and painted spruce boards pay homage to the forested lakefront. Honoring the classic A-frame design has allowed for a modern take on this three-season lakeside escape.

CHALET A

# The Future of Off-Grid Cuisine Lies in Past Tradition

Discover the trend of growing, cooking, and preserving food in ways that hearken to pre-electric traditions—while forging new paths.

**W**hat is off-grid cuisine? It's a term that's gained traction over the last few decades, but the definition isn't set in stone, and it's as long as a piece of kitchen string.

At its core, off-grid cuisine refers to any means of cultivating or preparing food that doesn't rely on electric power. Imagine searing freshly caught snapper over an open fire on the beach in Florida's tropical Everglades National Park. Or masterminding a vegan feast from your garden on a solar-powered kitchen stove at the upscale Three Rivers Recreation Area near the National Grasslands in Oregon. Or air-drying honeycomb-shaped morel mushrooms foraged in summer from the Great Smoky Mountains National Park in North Carolina, storing them to be used in cooler months to make a rich nutty broth.

The ways to grow and prepare food without power are as varied as the people who do so. It's estimated that there are 250,000 people living off-the-grid in the U.S., with some of the most popular states including New York, New Mexico, Utah, Florida, and California. People go off-grid for many reasons—economic, environmental, and for their mental health, among others. But when it comes to cuisine, off-grid is difficult to quantify. It includes everything from the food a homesteading family in Alaska might grow and eat to a pasta dinner prepared by friends on a solar-powered RV getaway in Joshua Tree.

What all off-grid cooking methods have in common is that they're all rooted in time-honored traditions spanning centuries and civilizations. The most ingenious, seemingly novel systems and techniques almost always rely on age-old, pre-grid understandings of the seasons and elements. Food management, of course, existed far before there was even an electricity grid to opt out of.

During summer visits to Saguaro National Park in Tucson, Arizona, you may encounter members of the Tohono O'odham Indigenous Nation harvesting fruits from the towering cacti, from which the park derives its name. The saguaro plant harvest was first recorded in 1540, but the Tohono O'odham, whose home has been in the region for thousands of years, have ways of life that predate colonial

Off-grid cooking can be as varied as searing freshly foraged food beach-side on an open grill or coming together to share a communally prepared meal.

"What all off-grid cooking methods have in common is that they're all rooted in time-honored traditions spanning centuries and civilizations."

documentation, including this anticipated yearly event. Using a pole fashioned from an aged saguaro stalk and up to 30 feet (9 meters) long—called a kuipad—the firm, pale green fruit pods at the tops of cacti are bumped off and retrieved down below. The fruit's bright red fibrous flesh is removed and separated from its black seeds, then boiled down over an open flame and dried in the sun to make jams and syrups. Some batches of syrup are fermented, and the wine is served in a Lunar New Year ceremony.

Today, renowned chefs like Tawnya Brant and Sean Sherman are revitalizing traditional indigenous approaches to cooking, including pre-grid methods and wild foods, at their high-profile restaurants and through educational initiatives. Numerous Indigenous nations have a rich tradition of air- and sun-drying vegetables like corn and squash, or preserving animal flesh for storage; for instance, placing fish over a flame protected by fresh branches to ensure it is carefully hot smoked. A popular concoction that's still made by many Indigenous nations is the pemmican—what could easily be described as the original energy bar. Composed of dried meat like bison and dried fruit such as cranberries, the mixture is broken down and rolled with rendered fat into portable, fortifying bars or balls that can last for years.

Perhaps one of the most famous off-grid innovators in the Western tradition is intrepid architect Michael Reynolds, an American no-waste trailblazer who constructed the first "Earthship" dwelling, endearingly called The Hobbit House, in the 1970s on a 630-acre (255-hectare) mesa in the desert north of Taos, New Mexico. This, along with earlier iterations of what would come to be known as "biotecture" structures, were made from bricks composed of scrap metal and foundations built from old tires. The basic Earthship design has developed over the decades, and there are now over 3,000 of them across the world, many in remote environments like the Canadian Prairies and the Fife peninsula in

Scotland. And while each Earthship is unique, many retain a fantasyland appearance.

Residents of these passive-solar-energy homes grow fruits and vegetables in greenhouses, usually abutting their kitchens; they cook food on thermal mass stoves that run on stored heat; and they keep provisions cool and dry in larders and root cellars—a preservation method that dates back tens of thousands of years. Current Earthship biotecture places great emphasis on growing food at home, including the use of vertical systems and suspended hydroponic planters. The Earthship Academy, where you can learn how to build your own biotecture habitat from adobe, stucco, cement, and glass bottles—plus those trusty aluminum cans and tires—also offers courses on food production.

Taking a pared-back approach, designer Mark Thorpe chose Upstate New York as the location to live his off-the-grid dream. In 2020, the recipient of the Green Good Design Award completed a minimalist black cedar structure in the Catskill Mountains, driven by the same desire to live harmoniously with nature that propelled transcendentalist Henry David Thoreau. During the 19th century, the Massachusetts-born naturalist had built his own small wood cabin and grew his own food—most likely corn, peas, and potatoes—famously documenting his two years of wild solitary living in what is now Walden Pond State Reservation, in 1854's *Walden*. Thorpe's 500-square-foot (46-square-meter)

design, called Edifice, is slightly larger in size, and divided into areas for living, cooking, eating, and sleeping. Though Edifice currently stands alone in the woods, it serves as a prototype for a 30-acre (12-hectare) natural sanctuary that contains similar structures—with potential for crops and gardening and replete with walking trails in a region known for its black trumpet, chanterelle, and chicken of the woods mushrooms.

Also harking back to the 19th century, the Fruita orchards in what is now the Capitol Reef National Park in Utah are a living testament to the region's agricultural past. In the 1880s, Mormon settlers planted thousands of fruit trees in the Fremont River Valley—a verdant gem amid a desert landscape, and to this day, pre-grid methods of cultivation

Residents of passive-solar-energy Earthship homes grow fruits and vegetables in greenhouses, while the farms of Cuyahoga Valley National Park practice sustainable agriculture.

are still used, including irrigation and plant-grafting techniques. The orchards are active, and visitors are encouraged to join the harvest, which runs from summer to fall. After a day of communal fruit picking, you're likely to leave with a hefty haul of apricots, peaches, cherries, pears, or apples.

In a similar spirit, the farms of Cuyahoga Valley National Park all practice sustainable agriculture—including many off- and pre-grid methods. The park's Countryside Initiative was started in 1999 to reinvigorate disused farmland on the park grounds. Today, Cuyahoga Valley boasts over twelve operational farms as a result of this effort. One of these is the 12-acre (4.9-hectare) Purplebrown farmstead, whose stewards subscribe to the tenets of permaculture, including the use of small and

> **"The ambition of Purplebrown famstead stewards is to maintain a diverse food forest, designed to simulate a naturally occurring ecosystem of fruits, vegetables, flowers, and mushrooms."**

slow solutions, producing no waste, using and valuing renewable resources, and catching and storing energy. Their ambition is to maintain a diverse food forest, designed to simulate a naturally occurring ecosystem of fruits, vegetables, flowers, mushrooms, and nuts. Meanwhile, at nearby Keleman Point Farm, you'll find rare breeds of animals raised naturally, including heritage turkeys for the pot and Tennessee Fainting goats whose cowskin-patterned coats are shorn to make cashmere.

While people living fully off the grid are, inevitably, difficult to access, many savvy off-grid cooks eagerly share their knowledge and experiences online. Sites like Off Grid Permaculture, Fresh Off the Grid, and Off Grid Tiny Vegan Homestead offer recipes, techniques, and tips on everything from intercropping and soil rotation to Kelly kettles and rocket stoves. These portals into the diverse lives of people making off-the-grid cuisine work are a good place to start for anyone curious to find out more about growing and preparing food without all the electric-powered trappings of modern life—whether the ambition is to try it out for a day or take up the challenge of a lifetime.

# Dedicated to Conserving the Great Smoky Mountains

BLACKBERRY FARM
GREAT SMOKY MOUNTAINS,
TENNESSEE

Opened in 1976 near the border of Great Smoky Mountains National Park, Blackberry Farm is a luxury resort rooted in its natural environment and renowned as a wellness destination with a Southern flair. What started as a six-room country inn has since expanded with the addition of 5,200 acres (2,104 hectares) of private land that make up Blackberry Mountain. The expanded property features elegant multi-bedroom cottages and mountaintop cabins made from locally sourced stone, and secluded treehouses tucked under the canopy of the surrounding forest.

An area covering 2,800 acres (1,133 hectares) of Blackberry Mountain has been dedicated to conservation, and in this private national park

setting, there is a seamless transition between indoor and outdoor spaces. Throughout the property, materials reflect a sense of place and culture, and dwelling spaces are simple but luxurious.

Intimate and cozy treehouses are cantilevered to make them feel as if they are floating in the treetops, and their white oak interiors are warmed by the light that spills in from the mountains. Tucked into the mountainside, the stone cottages feature walls of reclaimed wood and floor-to-ceiling windows to maximize views of the Great Smoky Mountains. Thanks to indoor and outdoor fireplaces, all seasons can be enjoyed here, but autumn is the park's particular gem when yellows and reds are caressed by layers of fog that the mountains are named after.

Perched on the peak of Blackberry Mountain, there is a restored 1950s lookout tower that boasts a 360-degree view. Other unique amenities include a library and an outdoor soaking tub. Beyond the daily hustle and bustle, Blackberry Mountain beckons travelers to embrace the tranquility of the Great Smoky Mountains and fully immerse themselves in the "Blackberry State of Mind."

BLACKBERRY FARM

GREAT SMOKY MOUNTAINS NATIONAL PARK

# Cultivating a Low-Impact Lifestyle

Like tending to a garden, fostering a sustainable way of life is all about taking cues from nature.

When contemplating the question of how to best build a lifestyle and dwelling that has minimal impact on the natural world, the short and long answer is: it depends. It depends on the landscape and climate; on the flora and fauna, and their unique relationship with the ecosystem; on the elements at play, and the way they shape daily life through sun, wind, and the chemistry of the soil itself. Perhaps most important is the realization that in spite of it all, there will be an impact. The question is, what kind of impact?

Living a sustainable lifestyle and translating that ethos to the home is not an easy task. In many ways, it requires constant self-assessment and a close relationship with the environment, almost like a system of checks and balances—if this, then that—in order to maintain a conscious awareness of the impact on both a macro and micro level. Just as the world turns, cycling through seasons and sunlight, nature never stops evolving and people shouldn't either. This perspective invites a closer look at the complexities of the natural world, an understanding that everything has a purpose and a place. With such stunning examples of perfect design, there are seemingly infinite ways one can find inspiration for everyday life.

"It's about taking cues from how things are naturally happening around you and designing systems that mimic that," says Dwyer

Haney of his 26-acre (10.5-hectare) permaculture farm in Northern Vermont. Haney discovered permaculture (a portmanteau for "permanent" and "agriculture") on a trip to Patagonia. He was fascinated by the way this holistic approach created a closed-loop system capable of generating resilient, nutrient-dense soil with very little waste by working harmoniously with the land, people, and animals. It led him to build a beautiful 400-square-foot (37-square-meter), off-grid timber frame home named Bending Birch Homestead on his farm where he and his family strive not only for a low but positive impact. The lumber for his tiny house came from a mill just five miles away.

"It's really small so it requires less energy, is insulated with sheep's wool, and heated by a

*This page:* Dwyer Haney's off-grid timber frame home in Northern Vermont, built with lumber from a local mill. *Opposite:* Hand-looming at Swannanoa Valley cabin.

"Living a sustainable lifestyle and translating that ethos to the home requires constant self-assessment and a close relationship with the environment."

natural surroundings. "Having a house that draws you out into the land is really important. That way, you aren't head down on your computer all day without realizing that there's a rainbow in front of you."

Without those windows and doors, it can be easy to forget about the rainbows. It's not hard to imagine how the many distractions of modern life can shift the collective focus to high-tech solutions and away from the mutually beneficial relationship between people and planet. If it is not reciprocal, it's simply not sustainable. What is good for one must be good for the other—or, from an ecological point of view—for many, *many* things. When it comes to 21st-century living, there is often more harm than good done to the land. Haney is adamant that sourcing local materials not only minimizes the impact but also allows those benefits to flow both ways.

"I try to build with materials from as close to here as possible to have the smallest environmental footprint possible, and I also try to use materials that will last a really long time, so they don't need to be replaced," says Haney. "The last piece is using materials that I can reuse, or my great-grandchildren can reuse."

Constructing a home with the intention of lasting for generations or being passed down

woodstove with firewood we cut on our property," explains Haney. "The most important thing is the woodstove. It heats the house, our hot water, but also has an oven. Using wood power is really important and helps us eschew a lot of fossil fuels and grid electricity." The homestead is designed around the principles of multipurpose elements and functionality. As a result, virtually all of their energy is generated naturally on-site, from solar panels that feed electricity directly to the home to gravity-fed spring water, and they take advantage of every opportunity to recycle nutrients back into the soil rather than letting them go to waste.

In terms of design, Haney sought out as many reclaimed windows and doors as possible to create a strong connection with the to posterity might not immediately appear synonymous with the zenith of low-impact living. However, Erin Gibbs, the Program Manager for the Brick Earth Stone and Timber (BEST) Workshop Preservation Program at the Historic Preservation Center in Grand Teton National Park, contends that it is precisely that. She goes on to suggest that our contemporary approach to housing often falls short in multiple aspects. Gibbs explains that according to research, people want to live in historic buildings. "There's something about the size, scale, and flow, and most of the time, they were deliberately designed in a way that was consistent and tried and true until the mass production of architecture in the 1960s," she says.

For Gibbs, what is "consistent and tried and true" are the artisanal building methods and natural materials employed (brick, mortar, wood, and stone) before today's homes began using cheaper, less durable, petrol-based products that were influenced more by trends and resale profits than longevity. History shows that this pivot to viewing a home as an asset, not a legacy meant to last generations, has a negative impact on people and the environment. Gibbs' efforts at the Grand Teton National Park is centered on educating others about why the parks system prioritizes preservation as evidenced by

*This page and opposite:* Scenes from Mike Belleme's Swannanoa Valley cabin and retreat in North Carolina (see pages 138–143), where almost everything was made by hand using local materials.

their maxim, "the greenest building is the one that's already built".

"These historic buildings by their very design, and the 'real' materials they use, are light on the landscape. So, when they can be reused and utilized in a way that leverages built-in sustainability, you end up with really low-impact living in these incredible places," says Gibbs. She also points out that tearing down an existing building condemns those materials to a landfill and will inevitably add more carbon to the atmosphere by extracting new materials and "restarting the whole cycle by using limited resources."

Unlike Haney and Gibbs, most people aren't stewarding a permaculture farm or preserving centuries-old buildings in a national park—they might not even own a home.

Nevertheless, several guiding principles can be distilled from these discussions to lead a more holistic and considerate way of life. As a dedicated grower, Haney advises eating locally grown seasonal produce that supports resilient, nutrient-dense soil in the area. "A lot of people don't really understand where their environmental impact comes from," says Haney. "Food is a really big area of impact, so I think it's good for people to understand where their impact is and attack the areas they think they can improve on the most. Sometimes, those areas are really surprising." He also encourages the use of a carbon footprint calculator to personally explore and understand this concept.

Like Haney, Gibbs champions using local building materials because they have an advantage as a low-impact, climate-resilient alternative to expensive, albeit cheaply made synthetic resources shipped from miles away. "Local materials have evolved to be in that environment." She gives the example of wood, which in its native environment has already learned how to manage factors like moisture, weather, and pests. "It doesn't even need to be painted, because it's still a tree performing as it was intended, but in a building," says Gibbs.

The many different threads woven into this larger tapestry of sustainable living are bound together by the importance of seeing the connection between all things, and the ripple effect of every action. To be a good steward is to take care of it all, both natural and man-made, in order to tread lightly and preserve the spaces and places that already exist. Perhaps the best way for us to live harmoniously is to always remind ourselves that humans and nature aren't separate entities but all integral parts of this ever-changing planet we call home.

**"It's good for people to understand where their impact is and attack the areas they think they can improve on the most. Sometimes, those areas are really surprising."**

# Modern Tranquility in Ohio's Scenic Amish Country

THE DWELL HOUSE
BY DWELLBOX
WALNUT CREEK, OHIO

Perched among the rolling hills of Holmes County, the Dwell House is an architectural tribute to Ohio's picturesque Amish Country. Designed and crafted by Jerry and Bethany Hershberger, this impressive endeavor by the former Amish duo mirrors the serenity of its environment. It masterfully blends rustic and industrial aesthetics, reminiscent of the architectural style associated with Frank Lloyd Wright. Constructed in 2018, the Dwell House beautifully captures the essence of the Hershbergers' Amish upbringing. Their exceptional carpentry skills infuse a unique architectural narrative into the house, skillfully reinterpreting traditional elements with a modern and innovative edge.

The house's cubic shape exudes a poised yet welcoming presence amidst the tranquil landscape. Utilizing Insulated Concrete Forms (ICF), the design fortifies the interior with concrete and a durable exterior of metal siding accentuated by mushroom wood inlays.

Inside, a blend of industrial aesthetics and organic tones awaits. Inspired by Wright's principles, an earthy palette pervades, featuring custom-built furniture by the Hershbergers. Elements like exposed steel trusses, as well as concrete floors and countertops, coexist with intricate woodwork, representing a modern rustic synthesis. The house's three levels align with the natural gradation of the hillside, which is studded with orderly rows of apple trees. Large windows stretching 10 feet (3 meters) high offer sweeping views of the encompassing landscape. From the valley's undulating hills to thriving orchards, nature is framed in a breathtaking panorama, even more stunning from the rooftop terrace that crowns the property. The home's sustainable design utilizes a private well for water and standard electricity. And the exterior mirrors the hues of the nearby parkland, seamlessly integrating the structure into its natural environment.

THE DWELL HOUSE BY DWELLBOX

THE DWELL HOUSE BY DWELLBOX

# A Puzzle-Box Cabin
# in the Swannanoa Valley
# of North Carolina

The Nook is a tranquil haven deeply rooted
in nature and the local community that invites
guests to live differently.

Checking in at Mike Belleme's jewel of a cabin
in the Swannanoa Valley involves taking a wind-
ing path through white oak and black walnut.
Unlike most trails, this one has been designed
to deliberately slow visitors down—the first
opportunity of many around The Nook to take
a breath and adjust to the rhythm of the natural
world. With that shift of perspective, Belleme's
bewitching sanctuary begins to reveal a trove of
unexpected details hidden away within its humble 400 square feet (37 square meters). "On the
outside, it's a pretty cabin," he says, "but if you
start to unpeel the layers, there are all these different stories to uncover." There's the intentionally impractical tea loft above the kitchen that
turns a morning brew into a miniature ceremony;
the locally crafted black walnut lacquer to match
the view of the black walnut tree; or the diorama
made with fur from the nest of a baby rabbit Belleme saved from the jaws
of a black snake while building his artful retreat.

Born in the mountains of Western North Carolina, Belleme grew up with
parents who shared a love of gardening and foraging, but it wasn't until
the photographer encountered the off-grid homestead Wild Roots, which
he chronicled for *National Geographic*, that he experienced something of
an epiphany. Committed to deepening their connection to the land, the
Wild Roots community has adopted many of the Earth skills innovated
by the Cherokee people who historically lived in the area. "I got really
thirsty for all that knowledge," says Belleme. "Learning how to make a fire

with friction, for example, you become really tapped into your surroundings. Being there was my wake-up call to the relationship between effort and connection and that became my guiding principle moving forward." Initially, that took the shape of living in a treehouse for three years with his now-wife Kristen, embracing the different pace of life and the upended priorities that ensued. They envisioned The Nook as an opportunity to share those experiences of more conscious, uncluttered living with others. What followed was a mammoth year-long build, "lying awake at night thinking about each decision and how it's going to affect another piece of the puzzle," says Belleme. "We have no regrets, but you have to be a little bit crazy to do this."

Fortunately, they didn't have to do it alone. About an hour's hike through the woods from The Nook is Lake Eden—the former site of Black Mountain College (1933–57), the pioneering communal experiment in arts education whose alumni include composer John Cage and artist Robert Rauschenberg. It's worth mentioning because Belleme's cabin is similarly the result of a community of artists pooling ideas, energy, and imagination—from the initial design to the artwork adorning the walls. "I can't say enough how much we leaned on community," Belleme says.

"Almost everything you can touch was made by hand, either by me, my friends, or people who are part of this community."

A pivotal partner in this endeavor was the creative duo from Asheville, Shelter Design Studio, who reshaped the cabin's blueprint according to Belleme's chance discoveries, from a salvaged arched window from Craigslist to the dead wood he unearthed in the forest and hauled to the sawmill. They brainstormed two distinct but complementary moods, both clean and minimalist: a light, Scandinavian aesthetic for the double-height front, complete with an indoor swing to appreciate the serene forest view and a more tucked-away Japanese dwelling in the lower half of the space. Outside, where Belleme has constructed a firepit and curving bathhouse, he planted native wild herbs, ferns, and black cohosh to promote a healthy forest. The result is a tranquil haven with deep roots in the local community. "We've had people say that the space had an impact on how they want to move through the world," he says. "It's a little window into what it feels like to live differently."

MIKE BELLEME/THE NOOK

# A Respectful Refresh of a Modernist Sonoma Coast Sea Ranch

A few hours north of San Francisco along the stunning Sonoma Coast lies The Sea Ranch—an iconic planned community with modernist architecture and a utopian spirit. One of the first houses in this progressive community sits tucked away in a redwood grove with no neighbors in sight. Originally designed by the famed architect Joseph Esherick, this modern house is emblematic of the 1960s idealism and experimental architecture that made the community famous.

The current owners—only the second since its original construction in 1968—sought a restoration and modernization that would respect the original layout and ethos. "Living lightly on the land" was an original

guiding principle of The Sea Ranch, inspired by the Indigenous Pomo people, and the same approach was used in this renovation led by Framestudio. The home's original plywood shelving was restored using reclaimed materials from the demolition, and materials like Douglas fir framing and redwood plywood siding capture the essence of the local coastal forest.

In the kitchen, natural rubber floors provide a clean and sophisticated look, accented by the warmer plywood and laminate cabinetry. Large windows connect the interior and exterior world with intimate views of the redwood forest that envelopes the house.

With the hum of the coastal waves in the distance, the modest 684-square-foot (64-square-meter) cabin spreads out over three levels, the original design embracing a utilitarian and low-cost aesthetic. The restoration sought to stay true to that energy, taking advantage of materials like plywood.

This sparse but compelling design is paired with the personal details and decor that pay homage to the cabin's original roots. Many of the mid-century furnishings are reflective of the era, like vintage Finnish pottery and a 1960s Japanese folding chair, all sourced secondhand.

MINI-MOD #3

MINI-MOD #3

# A Modern A-Frame Hidden Among Redwoods of Sonoma County

CAZ CABIN
CAZADERO, CALIFORNIA

Tucked away in the lush wilderness of Cazadero, California, the Caz Cabin reflects a lifelong dream of homeowners and architects Brit and Daniel Epperson. This tranquil hideaway blends seamlessly with its surrounding redwoods, offering a secluded retreat near the Russian River and Sonoma's legendary vineyards.

In 2014, the Eppersons began their project remodeling a 1974 A-frame cabin. By 2020, they had transformed the 1,088-square-foot (101-square-meter) space into a sanctuary echoing pastoral elegance. The exterior pays homage to the woodland surroundings, sporting redwood siding painted in black, resulting in a striking contrast to the neighboring parkland.

Inside, the space is thoughtfully defined with a geometric fireplace and balanced black kitchen features, while custom furnishings add a touch of rustic charm. To maximize natural light, the walls and ceiling were painted in light alabaster, reflecting sunlight that filters through the surrounding forest. This creates the effect of a "lantern of light in the middle of the woods," as Brit puts it, complemented by light European oak floors that warm up the all-white space.

The cabin's design honors the local environment, with materials selected to complement the woodland aesthetics and accommodate the climate. Its prime location offers mesmerizing views of the wilderness, inviting the owners to a life centered around the joys of nature.

Sustainability is at the core of the architectural blueprint, incorporating innovative solutions like rainwater collection and efficient waste management systems. Communal outdoor seating areas inspire connection, and a firepit becomes a gathering point on cool evenings.

The story of the Caz Cabin epitomizes architecture's potential to respect the environment and adapt to the locale. It showcases the Eppersons' architectural prowess, offering a glimpse into a private oasis amidst nature's majesty.

CAZ CABIN

CAZ CABIN

# Resurrecting a Remote Cabin Deep in the Angeles National Forest

SANTA ANITA CABIN
ANGELES NATIONAL
FOREST, CALIFORNIA

Though it is only an hour's drive to the San Gabriel Mountains from Los Angeles, once ensconced within its craggy wilderness and that of the Angeles National Forest, one feels worlds away from the big city. And that's exactly the appeal of Santa Anita Cabin for homeowner and film director Anthony Russo.

One of several cabins built in the 1900s as part of a U.S. Forest Service program to encourage responsible land use, Russo's stone-clad cottage is a tidy 600 square feet (56 square meters). But it would be a mistake to imagine a stuffy, dark space. Thanks to Commune Design, the team Russo hired to renovate the cabin, Santa Anita is all welcoming nooks and crannies, angled ceilings, and woods shined to a warm gloss amid snug reading corners and tucked-away sleeping lofts.

Commune sought inspiration from Swedish and French chalets as well as Japanese and Shaker designs, filtering it all through a pragmatic lens to adjust for the cabin's small footprint. This means the home's charm is found in scrumptious details like a sweet Dutch door à la Snow White with a bronze doorknob cast from local river rock. Other endearing features include finger joinery in the kitchen cabinets, a custom armoire from salvaged redwood, a stone fireplace, knotty cedar beams, and a crank telephone that rings only to neighboring cabins.

Santa Anita is fully off-grid. There is no sewage, no water, definitely no Wi-Fi or cell service. Electricity is sourced from truck batteries that harvest solar power, a shower room uses water from the creek, and an outhouse is equipped with a composting toilet. In fact, the home is so off-grid that accessing it requires a 40-minute hike through the canyon. Anything that needs to be transported to the cabin is either by hand, foot, or mule.

Everything about the place has a Robert Frost sensibility—where one can reset in solitude.

SANTA ANITA CABIN

# A Serene Canyon Oasis Encircled by Iconic California Parklands

CANYON PARKSIDE OASIS
RUSTIC CANYON,
CALIFORNIA

Amid the wild sprawl of canyons and coastlines on the western edge of Los Angeles, Canyon Parkside Oasis hides in a wooded hamlet dense with leafy sycamores and tangled oaks. As if in a children's fairy tale, the unassuming home seemingly appears out of nowhere.

It's clear the house was designed to mesh with the untamed nature that surrounds it. It reflects the best of indoor-outdoor living: trees sprout up through a deck beside a picnic table, cushy chairs swing from branches, and a netted hammock dangles between two palm trees. Elsewhere on the property, an icy stream gurgles down from a watershed in the mountain and collects in a natural soaking pool—a welcome treat on a hot summer day—and a walking path meanders through a native garden where bulbous mushrooms bloom from tree trunks after heavy rains and wildflowers perfume the air in spring.

Moving from Venice Beach to find peace amid nature, the homeowners have preserved an ethos of simplicity in keeping with the house's interior design. Crisp white walls and ceilings reflect the greenery outdoors, while the soft greens and velvety blues of the furniture and the natural woods complement it. In all the outdoor "rooms," woven blankets and thick, colorful rugs keep things cozy. Beyond the main house, a tidy yurt offers a breezy sleeping den amid "camp" fixtures like an archery range, tree swings, and a ping-pong table.

With a landscape teeming with life, Canyon Parkside Oasis could be its very own parkland. But it's actually just one small nook among thousands of acres of wild lands. It borders the 187-acre (76-hectare) Will Rogers State Park and the 153,000-acre (61,917-hectare) Santa Monica Mountains National Recreation Area, where nearly 500 miles (805 kilometers) of hiking trails thread deep into canyons, high into mountains, and along pristine beaches.

CANYON PARKSIDE OASIS

# Working and Living Off-Grid and on the Move

The advent of remote employment has ignited our collective imagination about what's possible when we take our home office on the road.

Late in 2020, copywriter and freelance journalist Mekenna Malan answered work emails and caught up on deadlines while snacking on cherry turnovers at a café in Ojai, California. Malan didn't actually reside in Ojai; in fact, she and her partner were simply passing through in their 1986 Land Cruiser-cum-camper van. They had popped into the café to log a few hours of work before driving through sun-dappled orange groves to an idyllic spot for dinner cooked on the Cruiser's tailgate.

Ojai was just one stop on Malan's 7,000-mile (11,265-kilometer) road trip around the United States. She detailed this 86-day adventure in an article for *Business Insider,* writing of the challenges of work-from-anywhere employment—a makeshift office comprising a laptop balanced on her knees, a passenger-side seat, and unreliable Internet—and also noting its perks. Like sunrise hikes before conference calls and a shifting landscape to fuel her creativity. As she explained in the article: Wi-Fi was spotty. But the views were epic.

Malan is one of thousands of people opting for an on-the-road or deep-in-nature lifestyle, one with the ability to work full-time from any place on Earth. Though this has been a growing trend since the mid- to late-2000s, the COVID-19 pandemic hastened matters. A Pew Research Center survey found that 59 percent of U.S. workers say their jobs can be accomplished outside of a traditional office. This is compared to 23 percent who reported the same thing pre-pandemic. And according to Upwork, by 2025, it is possible that 32.6 million Americans (about 22 percent of the workforce) will be employed remotely.

Desire for a flexible schedule, a curiosity for new places, a need to be in nature, greater access to outdoor recreation, and a cheaper cost of living: these are all reasons people choose to live and work outside of urban and suburban areas.

Sndividuals like Malan choose to establish their mobile base in vans, RVs, or converted vehicles, enabling them to dine, rest, work, and explore, all while on the move. Social media influencer Shilletha Curtis relies on her own two feet, hiking the Continental Divide

For people working remotely, often a laptop and Wi-Fi are all that's needed, while breathtaking views can give creative workers the inspiration they need.

"For some remote workers, 'home' can be a new destination every few days, and 'offices' are coffee shops, visitor centers, public libraries, laundromats, or even craggy mountain peaks."

and working from forested slopes and flat-top mesas. For these folks, "home" is a new destination every few days, and "offices" are coffee shops, visitor centers, public libraries, laundromats, or even craggy mountain peaks. For people in creative industries, who require quiet time to think and work, living and working remotely are often the perfect bedfellows. Filmmakers, artists, writers, designers, agency creatives: all are able to work in homes adjacent to nature as long as there is Wi-Fi on-site or close by, dipping back into the metropolitan centers of their respective industries when needed. For many, being away from those metropolitan centers is what gives them the headspace to fully engage with their work. Plenty of other desk-based jobs can be managed in much the same way.

Some people find themselves suited to seasonal jobs—park rangers, mountain guides, ski instructors, outdoor educators, park lodge employees—that transport them to different parts of the country for a work-centered adventure. Consider the artist Lauren Carlson who road-tripped from Memphis to Moab in spring 2023 to take a resort gig in southern Utah's otherworldly red rocks. Or Jonathan Baxter, who has traveled to national parks like Acadia, Zion, Yellowstone, and Joshua Tree as a trail builder, a job that often leads him into deep backcountry, with mail delivered by mules his only connection to the outside world. The beautifully detailed Trail Crew Stories project documents the day-to-day lives of Baxter and people like him.

For social media influencer and river guide Kiya Echohawk, there is also the allure of tapping into something larger than herself. She said in a profile published by Parks Project: "Being a part of the outdoor community has so many benefits when it comes to connecting with others who have similar interests…The sense of belonging to a greater community has enriched my experiences and provided opportunities for learning and growth." Being part of a community, for some remote dwellers, can also mean sharing workspaces and pooling resources, whether it's a purpose-built studio on a private property or meeting in a local café to bounce ideas around and generally feel part of a working environment, however casual.

It's not just river guiding, trail building, and freelance telework that lends itself to remote work-life. Cottage and craft industries such as potting, woodworking, textile production, as well as co-op farming, allow people the opportunity for non-traditional living and working. For example, the 244.5-acre (99-hectare) non-profit farm Sustainable Settings, in Carbondale, Colorado, offers short-term and long-term apprenticeships where workers eat, sleep, work, and live on-site. At Singing Cedars Farmstead in Vermont's Champlain Valley, Scott Greene and Rebecca Maden grow vegetables in their greenhouse year-round and invite guests to live and learn on the property via apprenticeships. Individuals typically apply for these through Worldwide Opportunities on Organic Farms (WWOOF), a social network and organization that links visitors with organic farmers in order to "promote an education exchange and build a global community conscious of ecological farming practices."

This isn't a new concept, however. There are several historical antecedents of retreats that blossomed into full-blown creative spaces or utopian endeavors, some still thriving to this day. One of them, Druid Heights, was

Specially designed office spaces in cabins and cottages are important to some, while communal work spaces help others to feel part of a shared working environment.

a mid-century artists' community in Marin County, California, founded by Elsa Gidlow and Roger Somers, who refashioned an old homestead ranch into a bohemian enclave that attracted the likes of Dizzy Gillespie, Lily Tomlin, poet Gary Snyder, and more. The National Parks Service manages the property now, although it has fallen into disrepair.

In 1970, in the Arizona desert, the experimental community Arcosanti was built and is still in operation today. Envisioned as a place for frugal living with a small environmental footprint, Acorsanti bills itself as "a prototype arcology, integrating the design of architecture with respect to ecology."

Scientists and researchers frequently collaborate in remote settings like parklands or the Mount Washington Observatory in New

Hampshire; Niwot Ridge Mountain Research Station in Colorado, a leading research center studying the impact of climate change on alpine ecosystems; and Haleakala Observatory in Maui, located 10,000 feet (3,048 meters) above sea level and considered one of the most important observatories in the world.

Furthermore, Native Americans have engaged in a type of "coworking" for countless generations—from hunting and foraging to trading and fostering communal bonds—and they've been doing so on lands from which they were forcibly removed and killed to make way for colonization. (It is important to note that the Haleakala Observatory is perched on a mountain that local Hawaiians consider sacred, and where they actively do not want an observatory.)

This prompts the question: What effects can be attributed to the remote work revolution and the growth of digital nomadism? On the one hand, it can help us more deeply engage with our wild lands, inspiring pro-conservation attitudes and environmental activism. It can also bring commerce and culture to struggling rural regions. On the other hand, an influx of visitors to ecologically sensitive areas and sacred sites can lead to over-tourism, harm to ecosystems, a reduced housing supply—and more expensive housing—for locals, and gentrification.

As with any emerging and evolving phenomenon, the impact is intricate and may not be readily evident. Shared work and living spaces, especially in remote wilderness and on parklands, can galvanize a spirit of collaboration. And collaboration is, and will be, key to not only problem-solving but also finding a synergy between newcomers and the local communities in which new arrivals make their temporary and permanent homes.

Relocating to remote areas can indeed generate tension. But it can also open the door for an exchange of ideas between people from diverse cultures, backgrounds, and industries, pooling resources and learning to cohabit—ideally, cooperatively—in innovative and surprising ways.

# A Dome Home Perched in the Santa Monica Mountains

GEODESIC DOME
TOPANGA, CALIFORNIA

The Santa Monica Mountains rise north of Los Angeles, a coastal mountain range dotted with sage and chaparral that slopes to salt marshes before reaching the Pacific Ocean. Centuries ago, native Tongva people named the area *topanga:* "where the mountain meets the sea." Today, Topanga Canyon is a tranquil escape from buzzy L.A. surrounded by the Santa Monica Mountains National Recreation Area, Malibu Creek State Park, and Topanga State Park.

Atop a sunlit canyon hill, you'll find Nick Fouquet's Geodesic Dome perched on a steep road. The hatmaker-to-the-stars (David Beckham, Jennifer Lopez, Pharrell Williams) unearthed the 1970s custom-crafted treasure in 2016. With help from Timothy McCarthy of Forma Design Group, a meticulous five-year restoration commenced.

To take advantage of the dome's vertical height and rounded edges—no 90-degree angles here—the team removed the interior walls throughout the three-story structure. Opening up the space created volume, offering an expansive flow and bringing in loads of natural light. The team also worked with designers to create custom furniture suited to the dome's shape.

Within the 1,800-square-foot (167-square-meter) home there's a bedroom-bathroom suite on the lower level, a kitchen and sitting area on the main level, and a loft with a living room and fireplace on the upper level. All are bathed in sunlight from triangular windows, which also help regulate heat. Two wraparound exterior decks enjoy north- and south-facing canyon views ideal for taking in California's pink sunsets.

Elsewhere on the one-acre (0.40-hectare) property is a swimming pool, a guest house, and a garden of fruit trees plump with lemons, limes, figs, apples, avocados, plums, and grapefruit. Fouquet calls the dome home, and also his sanctuary, an oasis caught somewhere between mountain and sea.

# An Architectural Ode to Washington's Wilderness

HIGH PRAIRIE RESIDENCE
LYLE, WASHINGTON

In Lyle, Washington's High Prairie community, the High Prairie Residence stands as a minimalist masterpiece within its 120-acre (49-hectare) rustic landscape. EB Architecture + Design built the house in 2019 with two key goals: to harmonize with the dramatic environment and offer simple comfort. These principles shine through everything, from the home's location, geometric design, and room layout to lighting, structure, and materials, resulting in a retreat that beautifully integrates with the wilderness, balancing simplicity and rugged charm. Owners Carl and Tori envisioned the house, affectionately known as the "blip on the hill," to honor the property's topography and respond to the surroundings.

Nestled into a gentle hillside, the home mirrors the region's agricultural aesthetic with an exterior of ground face concrete blocks and a weathering steel roof. Two site walls extend the structure's west face, fortifying it against the wind and serving as an organic extension of the landscape. The interior is divided into public and private areas by a central site-cast concrete wall. Polished concrete floors provide a sleek yet sturdy finish throughout the house, and large windows create an abundance of natural light. The primary suite descends from the main level, forming a secluded haven enriched by 360-degree views. Two additional bedrooms and a shared bath form the guest suite, tucked away in their own corner of the residence. A covered communal outdoor space and an inviting entry court balance the solidity of the adjacent bedroom suites, drawing in the exterior landscape.

The High Prairie Residence celebrates honest durability, letting the setting's natural drama take center stage. It successfully merges functionality and aesthetics, respecting and mirroring the varied topography, plant life, and wildlife of its rural backdrop while offering views of the distant volcanic peaks of the Cascade Range and the rolling hills of Columbia Gorge.

HIGH PRAIRIE RESIDENCE

# A Sanctuary in Harmony
# with the Vast Sonoran Desert

TUCSON MOUNTAIN
RETREAT
TUCSON, ARIZONA

Nestled against the borders of Saguaro National Park, the Tucson Mountain Retreat is a striking example of architecture in communion with nature. Designed by architects Cade Hayes and Jesus Robles of DUST, the building is composed of elemental materials forming a sanctuary in harmony with its rugged desert surroundings.

The retreat stretches across an expanse of land dotted with local flora and fauna, all under the watchful gaze of majestic saguaro cacti. Its walls, shaped from compressed earth, exude permanence and merge effortlessly with the surrounding landscape. When the desert light washes over them, their earthen textures come alive. The dwelling is separated into distinct zones, each reflecting a unique aspect of the desert, from the raw, terrestrial beauty of the desert floor to the celestial canopy above.

Home to two doctors, the retreat is custom designed to reflect their lifestyle and deep love for music. The layout facilitates sound flow and isolation, while Spanish cedar infuses private areas with a rich aroma. Broad glass panels blur the line between interior and exterior, revealing the home's dual orientation to the north and south. From the exterior passages to the panoramic roof deck, the retreat encourages an immersive interaction with the desert environment. Solar energy powers the retreat's utilities, enhancing its self-sufficiency and reducing its environmental impact. Rainwater collection systems ensure water sustainability, while gravity-fed showers maintain an off-grid lifestyle. The garden reflects the flora of the desert landscape, and a firepit fosters a sense of community, reinforcing the dwelling's harmonious integration with the surrounding parkland.

The Tucson Mountain Retreat is more than just a house—it's an extension of the desert, a sanctuary carved from the landscape. Architecture and nature entwine in a symphony, transforming living into an immersive sensory experience.

TUCSON MOUNTAIN RETREAT

# A Tiny House in the Big Heart of Texas Hill County

ELSEWHERE CABIN A
GEORGETOWN, TEXAS

About half an hour from the bustling capital of Austin in Texas Hill County, a tiny refuge on an idyllic ranch provides the perfect spontaneous getaway from the city. Surrounded by horses, longhorns, and other Texas wildlife, the focus of this off-the-grid tiny house is the sense of calmness and serenity that comes from being in harmony with the natural surroundings. The mobile cabin, built on a trailer bed, seamlessly blends the indoors and outdoors. Open the 10-foot (3-meter) folding door that extends along one wall and turn the whole living space into a porch. Sit directly on the deck, or if the weather changes, step inside and take in the view from the comfort of the couch. With its dark, charred cedar siding—

done on-site by hand—the cabin sits elegantly perched, ready for taking in sunsets over the hills and oak trees.

One side of the cabin is slightly inset, with a fiberglass door revealing storage space for the solar-powered water heater, propane tank, and ample firewood for a bonfire. While the tiny house is built with disconnection in mind, if work calls, there's even solar-powered Wi-Fi. The considered interior furnishings make the modest space feel luxurious. Warm plywood walls contrast with black interlocking rubber tiles. A ladder climbs to the suspended sleeping space above, which features a cozy double bed. On the main level a singular surface transitions from desk to sofa to kitchen counter. While intimate and perfect for a romantic getaway, the cabin can accommodate an extra person, as the downstairs sofa can be turned into a bed. A frosted glass wall between the kitchen and bathroom provides privacy while distributing light throughout the small space.

The motto in this state might be "everything's bigger in Texas" but this tiny cabin begs to differ. Its small cozy spaces feel just right and exude the tranquility that comes from being at one with the larger-than-life Texas countryside.

# A Hideout a Stone's Throw from Iconic Desert Parklands

FOLLY JOSHUA TREE
JOSHUA TREE, CALIFORNIA

Joshua Tree National Park spans the vast Mojave and Colorado deserts. Skirting the edges of the park, two structures—their steel walls weathered dusky—loom like a mirage. The architectural forms are simple: square with pitched roofs. But like any good mirage, the truth is revealed only upon closer inspection. At Folly Joshua Tree, the interiors of these cabins, seemingly frozen in time, now feature modern, self-sustaining homes.

Finished in 2018 by architectural designer Malek Alqadi, Folly runs on solar power stored on-site and filters its own water with blackwater and greywater systems. Innovative technology monitors energy consumption, offers controlled secure entry, and automates light settings. Interior temperatures

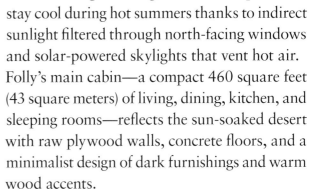

stay cool during hot summers thanks to indirect sunlight filtered through north-facing windows and solar-powered skylights that vent hot air.

Folly's main cabin—a compact 460 square feet (43 square meters) of living, dining, kitchen, and sleeping rooms—reflects the sun-soaked desert with raw plywood walls, concrete floors, and a minimalist design of dark furnishings and warm wood accents.

In the second cabin, nicknamed "Stargazing," the aesthetic continues with a roofless second-story bedroom for clear sky views. Oriented toward the North Star, this open-air room is accessed by outdoor stairs, and is kitted with a bio-ethanol fireplace and heated bed to ward off the nighttime desert chill.

Alqadi drew inspiration from the sense of illusion one experiences in the desert, where what appears to be barren—like horizons of sand—is actually thriving with life.

The feature most reminiscent of Folly's stark desert environs is the steel skin enveloping the cabins' exteriors. It was shimmery silver when first put on, but over time, it has responded to the blazing sun, pelting rain, and gusting winds—shifting its texture and color endlessly, so it never looks the same way twice.

FOLLY JOSHUA TREE

JOSHUA TREE NATIONAL PARK

# A Cozy Oasis with Sweeping Mojave Desert Views

THE SHACK ATTACK
JOSHUA TREE, CALIFORNIA

A 1950s cabin decaying in the Mojave Desert was last on Brian and Kathrin Smirke's list of real estate to purchase. They already owned two properties in Joshua Tree, the quirky town near Joshua Tree National Park they had come to love as their retreat from the bustle of Los Angeles. Though this cabin was in the same desirable area, it had to be stripped to the studs and completely rebuilt to make it habitable. It seemed overwhelming. But in 2015, as they watched their other choices go to top bidders at auction, the Smirkes suddenly found themselves the owners of a parcel of land that would become The Shack Attack.

The couple spent nearly two years reimagining and reconstructing the

480-square-foot (45-square-meter) house. With the music of Roy Orbison, John Coltrane, and Charles Bradley playing in the background, the Smirkes did all the work themselves—from design and demolition to framing, plumbing, and art (like a sunny stained-glass window, a sleep lamp, a striking wall hanging).

Building codes meant Brian and Kathrin couldn't expand the home's footprint, a challenge that unleashed their creativity. They customized furniture to precise dimensions to fit the space perfectly. They jackhammered the concrete to plant an interior cactus garden. They added a wall, a move that might seem counterintuitive in a home the size of a studio, but one that allowed for more defined living spaces. And they changed the orientation of the front and back doors, reversing the two so that upon entering, one gazes instantly at the huge windows that outline a sweep of desert rolling to the horizon. In fact, nothing in Shack Attack blocks these ends-of-the-Earth sightlines, but the best place to soak it all up is outside. The Smirkes constructed a custom outdoor tub from which one can see Joshua Tree's famed rock formations, ancient creosote bushes, and the inky night sky studded with stars and galaxies.

THE SHACK ATTACK

SONORAN DESERT NATIONAL MONUMENT

# A Retreat Designed to Honor Nature and Withstand Wildfires

CAMPOUT
LAKE TAHOE, CALIFORNIA

Built for a San Francisco-based family near Lake Tahoe in the Sierra Nevada Mountains, this mountain retreat celebrates the beauty of nature but also deeply understands its realities. In recent years, this has become one of the epicenters of wildfires, and the highly considered design of this space hinges on addressing some of the potential risks of the local environment. From the outside, the building has a concrete, box-like structure. Concrete and steel sash tempered windows form a fire-resistive barrier and help to secure a native cedar interior that is left unfinished. While many houses look out, this one looks in. Glazing is minimized on the exterior, and instead, focused on the interior courtyard. With the rest of the building

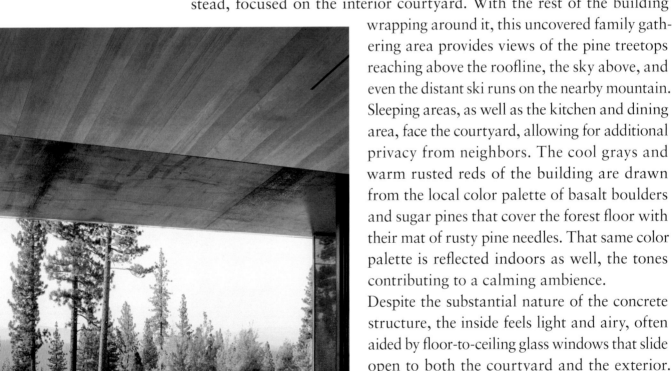

wrapping around it, this uncovered family gathering area provides views of the pine treetops reaching above the roofline, the sky above, and even the distant ski runs on the nearby mountain. Sleeping areas, as well as the kitchen and dining area, face the courtyard, allowing for additional privacy from neighbors. The cool grays and warm rusted reds of the building are drawn from the local color palette of basalt boulders and sugar pines that cover the forest floor with their mat of rusty pine needles. That same color palette is reflected indoors as well, the tones contributing to a calming ambience.

Despite the substantial nature of the concrete structure, the inside feels light and airy, often aided by floor-to-ceiling glass windows that slide open to both the courtyard and the exterior. This creates one seamless flow from exterior to interior and out again.

As dwellings and developments extend further and further into wild spaces subject to wildfires, all exacerbated by climate change, this house is proof of what it takes to consider the local environment and potential threats, and to design in a way that doesn't shy away from the facts on the ground.

CAMPOUT

# A Modern Haven Nestled in Colorado's Rocky Mountains

BIG CABIN | LITTLE CABIN
FAIRPLAY, COLORADO

Perched amid the windswept crags of Fairplay, Colorado, Big Cabin | Little Cabin reinterprets the classic log cabin with a modernist design twist. Brought to life by Renée del Gaudio Architecture, this pair of stunning cabins stands majestically on a cliff's edge, with the tranquil Sangre de Cristo Mountains providing a breathtaking backdrop.

The twin cabins command sweeping views of the horizon and the rolling landscape. Their strategic placement shelters a quaint space in between, where a solitary mature pine graces the deck, fusing the structure with its lush surroundings. The design incorporates rustic cedar siding and traditional gabled roofs, paying homage to the region's vernacular archi-

tecture, while the plywood interiors carry the tranquil rural theme.

Colombian artist Maricel Blum envisioned the space, which serves as both her creative sanctuary and ski haven. The interiors are defined by expansive glass windows. As sunlight permeates the cabins, it casts a dynamic canvas of shadows and light across the rustic interiors. Every window frames a distinctive perspective on the landscape, from the imposing mountains to the sun-dappled forests that blanket the valley below.

The cabins' design and material selection reveal a deep respect for their surroundings. The dark-stained exteriors merge harmoniously with the neighboring woods, creating an eco-conscious aesthetic. Sustainability is at the core of their design, featuring closed-cell foam insulation, triple-pane Low-E glass windows, and an ultra efficient boiler. Solar panels generate the cabins' electricity, allowing off-grid living without compromising sustainability.

Big Cabin | Little Cabin embodies a simplicity that allows nature to take center stage. Here, the undisturbed beauty of the wilderness and the calming solitude harmonize to craft the perfect retreat for an artist seeking inspiration.

# A Cliff-Hugging A-Frame With a Zion National Park Panorama

ZION ECO CABIN
HILDALE, UTAH

Sipping coffee on the deck of Zion Eco Cabin in the early morning, one might spot a golden eagle or a hawk slicing through the azure Utah sky. Or, peering below the deck's high perch, one can see deer or ring-tailed cats—a cougar even—roaming the canyon floor. No matter where your gaze rests, nature captivates the experience.

This was the intent of owners Lee and Mindy Barlow when they designed the 144-square-foot (13-square-meter) A-frame. The Barlows structured the house so that each line of sight deliberately guides the view to the landscape, framing nature's artwork.

Set in the pink-hued rocks of the Canaan Mountains on the southeast boundary of Zion National Park, the home's location is surrounded by nearly 45,000 acres (18,211 hectares) of pristine wilderness. This is a place where eons of wind and water have sculpted blocks of Navajo sandstone, delicate arches, and slim slot canyons; where plateaus wear crowns of ponderosa pines and juniper, and sagebrush stud the mountains; and where seeps in the canyon walls nourish hanging gardens of monkeyflower and maidenhair fern. The A-frame welcomes this wild nature indoors via an entire wall that louvers up, opening the interior space to a wide-planked deck. Stairs lead to a lower deck and then to a bottom-level patio where an energy-efficient eco-spa sits—the spot to enjoy the glittering nighttime celestial sights.

The Barlows integrated the staircases and decks to seamlessly meld with the undulating contours of the cliffside, and the decor pays homage to the terrain, too, with layered textures and vibrant colors set against a palette of tawny tans and creamy beiges. Most of the external facade of the home finds its origins in repurposed materials, a testament to the Barlows' commitment to harmonizing the construction of Zion Eco Cabin with conservation and resourcefulness.

223

ZION ECO CABIN

ZION ECO CABIN

# An Iconic Coastal Dwelling from an Ecological Master Planner

LAWRENCE HALPRIN'S
SEA RANCH
THE SEA RANCH,
CALIFORNIA

One of the most notable landscape architects of the 20th century, Lawrence Halprin helped to change how people experience urban space. His best-known design might just have been his most personal: the infamous 1960s planned community along the Sonoma Coast, The Sea Ranch. Commissioned to create a master plan for this tract of 5,000 acres (2,023 hectares), Halprin was deeply connected to the land that he worked with, inspired by his own commitment "to inhabit this land and protect the awesome character without softening or altering it." Like many involved in the creation of this innovative experiment in ecological design, Halprin also owned his own home in the celebrated coastal landscape.

The original cabin was destroyed after a fire in 2001. When rebuilt, the new building was designed almost exactly like the original, and the 2,123-square-foot (197-square-meter) L-shaped house embodies the quintessential Sea Ranch style. The building's weathered cedar siding and Douglas fir trim blend into the surrounding landscape. Natural materials are just as important on the inside, with its warm wood paneling and rough rock for the kitchen counter and fireplace. The open floor plan is accentuated by varying ceiling heights, creating stark angles. Windows frame every view, capturing micro-moments of the world outside. On the back deck, a solarium welcomes in the coastal views and light. From there, the deck leads to a small amphitheater for evening bonfires overlooking the ocean where Halprin's wife, a professional dancer, once led workshops.

It's the only home in the entire Sea Ranch community to be built right at the edge of the bluffs, an architectural overhang that over time has become a part of the landscape itself. The design is a testament not just to Halprin's legacy but also to the potential of buildings and communities that seek to create a symbiotic relationship with their environment.

LAWRENCE HALPRIN'S SEA RANCH

# Minimalist Style Meets Off–Grid Living in This Ever–Changing Maui Home

Graham Hill designed a stylish 1,000-square-foot (93-square-meter) home that shapeshifts in novel ways to function like a house twice its size.

The urban lifestyle of Manhattan and the laid-back living of Maui share nothing in common—on the surface, that is. It was city life—or more specifically, the tiny footprint of city apartments—that led Graham Hill to create LifeEdited Maui, a small home that leaves a big impression.

An internet tech and business entrepreneur, Hill had been living in New York City in a spacious loft in the 2000s. By the time he sold his successful sustainability and design website TreeHugger in 2007, Hill had created a virtual office where all employees worked remotely, including himself. He traveled the world, soon realizing how little one needs to not only survive but also thrive. In 2010, he launched LifeEdited, a development firm that designs hyper-efficient, small-scale homes with moving parts—think sliding walls and expandable furniture—and subsequently debuted the prototype for LifeEdited Maui. It was called LifeEdited 1, and it was a 420-square-foot (39-square-meter) studio in Manhattan that performed like a space much larger than its dimensions. "We gain a lot when we go small," Hill says. "It's all about smart, flexible design."

LifeEdited 1 (LE1) inspired LE2, an even smaller unit in the same building, and eventually LifeEdited Maui (LEM). Hill's cousin had lived on Maui for 20 years, and on one of his frequent visits to her place in Haiku, she offered to sell Hill a few acres of her land. Hill's goal was to create a structure based on tiny home design principles that was off-grid and had minimal environmental impact.

Completed in 2018, the LEM features four bedrooms and 2.5 bathrooms and feels like a house twice its size with defined spaces and lots of flow. Hill partnered with Hawaii Off-Grid for the project and used Clei transformable furnishings from Resource Furniture for pieces that fold, expand, swivel, and stack. For example, two bedrooms have Murphy beds, one with an attached desk that rotates into place when the bed is closed, and the living space has low coffee tables that pop up into dining tables, and modular sofas with back cushions that are upright when used as dining chairs and reclined when it's time to relax.

As for LEM's ability to be off-grid, Hill employed green tech such as a standing seam metal roof with Sunflare thin-film solar panels, which generate enough power to run the entire house. The roof's gutters channel water into a tank, and solar thermal panels affixed to it circulate the home's hot water source sans electricity. And LEM's Separett composting toilets require zero water.

Additional green features include an antifungal paint for the walls, which eliminates most, if not all, air pollution, a kitchen backsplash made from eco-friendly paper, north-facing windows, and edible landscaping.

Then there's the lanai. Offering 330 square feet (31 square meters) of open-air living space, the lanai—as anyone who's visited a tropical locale knows—is the heart of island life. It's also the unique quality of LEM that Hill wasn't able to execute in New York's LE1 and LE2. "There was experimentation from LE1 to LE2, and I learned from it," Hill explains. "LEM had very different design parameters, including that it was in a temperate environment. The lanai expands the space exponentially."

Hill hopes his LifeEdited houses will serve as prototypes for future homes for others. In fact, that mission is key to his latest venture, The Carbonauts, which guides people towards compelling, low-footprint ways of living and working. Because it's good for the planet, yes—but also, as Hill aptly says, "A smaller life is a happier life."

GRAHAM HILL/LIFEEDITED MAUI

243

# A Tropical Refuge Inspired by Florida Modernist Principles

BRILLHART HOUSE
MIAMI, FLORIDA

How do you design a space where you don't just look at the landscape but are fully immersed within it? That was the driving question behind this modern tropical refuge built to minimize impact and to work in conjunction with the local climate and landscape.

When an architect couple stumbled upon an empty lot in one of Miami's oldest neighborhoods, they embraced the principles of mid-century Florida modernism, drawing inspiration from the local landscape, climate, and materials to shape their design.

The result is a breezy, modern refuge with a relaxing oasis feel. Because of the deep lot, the couple chose to elevate the building off the ground, creating a sense of floating among the lush foliage. To meld the interior and exterior, uninterrupted glass spans the length of both sides of the house. The outdoor areas extend the living space, with front and back porches. Wood shutters along the front welcome in balmy breezes and play with the sun to project striking patterns.

Brillhart House, with its compact 1,500 square foot (139 square meter) footprint, was meticulously built to minimize its environmental impact. Challenging the more conventional use of concrete, the superstructure was instead made of steel and glass. This design and construction process helped to minimize waste and simplify assembly, and the innovative use of materials also allows for increased cross ventilation—essential in the tropical Florida climate.

In the flashiness of Miami, the building's more modest profile and size set it apart. Like all houses, this one is part of a larger ecosystem. Situated along the Miami River, which drains out of the local Everglades National Park, the neighborhood is largely defined by its mature tree canopy. Additional landscaping was done to emphasize that dense and lush feel. The result is a modernist marvel, a secluded floating tropical refuge embedded into the verdant landscape.

BRILLHART HOUSE

BRILLHART HOUSE

pp. 132–137
Architecture:
Jerry Hershberger
Interior Design:
Bethany Hershberger
Photography:
Shelby Wilray
@shelbywilray

## THE SHACK ATTACK

Joshua Tree, California
pp. 204–209
@the_shack_attack
Architecture:
We Are In Our Element
weareinourelement.com
Photography:
Brian Smirke
@briansmirke

## TIVOLI BARN

Tivoli, New York
pp. 8–13
@thebarnintivoli
Photography:
Alon Koppel Photography
alonkoppel.com

## TRUE NORTH CABIN

Eagle Harbor, Michigan
pp. 98–101
truenorthcabin.com
Photography:
Bryana Palosaari,
Lynn Makela, Jason Makela

## TUCSON MOUNTAIN
RETREAT

Tucson, Arizona
pp. 186–189
tucsonmountainretreat.com
Architecture:
DUST
dustdb.com
Photography:
Bill Timmerman
billtimmerman.com

## ZION ECO CABIN

Hildale, Utah
pp. 222–229
@zionecocabins
Photography:
Ethan Abitz
ethanabitz.com

# ADDITIONAL
MOOD IMAGES

pp. 6–7:
Kenny McCartney/
Getty Images
pp. 20–21:
Deb Snelson/
Getty Images
pp. 40–41:
James Michael House/
Getty Images
pp. 72–72:
Bkamprath/
Getty Images
pp. 86–87:
RnDmS/
Getty Images
pp. 94–95:
Melissa Kopka/
Getty Images
pp. 124–125:
matejphoto/
Getty Images
pp. 158–159:
franckreporter/
Getty Images
pp. 202–203:
yongyuan/
Getty Images
pp. 208–209:
Thomas Roche/
Getty Images
pp. 244–245:
Pierre Leclerc Photography/
Getty Images

# Parklife Hideaways

## COTTAGES AND CABINS IN NORTH AMERICAN PARKLANDS

This book was conceived and edited by gestalten and Parks Project

Design and layout by gestalten in cooperation with Parks Project

Edited by Robert Klanten and Laura Allsop
Contributing editors: Parks Project
Editorial support by Effie Efthymiadi and Joe Gibson

Introduction by Keith Eshelman

Texts by Tanner Bowden (pp. 43–49), Anna Brones (pp. 9–33, 51–57, 67, 81, 99–107, 119, 145, 191, 211, 231, 247), Katherine Englishman (pp. 127–131), Jessica Dunham (pp. 61, 97, 161–177, 197–205, 223, 239-240), Hannah Lack (pp. 75–76, 89–90, 139–140), Kevin Oberbauer (pp. 133, 153, 181–187, 217), and Ananda Pellerin (pp. 113–117)

Editorial Management by Lars Pietzschmann

Design, layout, and cover by Stefan Morgner

Photo Editor: Zoe Paterniani

Typefaces: Migra by Valerio Monopoli, Sabon by Jan Tschichold

Cover photography by Studio North Inc/studionorth.ca
Backcover photography by Ethan Abitz/ethanabitz.com

Printed by Printer Trento S. r. l., Trento
Made in Europe

Published by gestalten, Berlin 2023
ISBN 978-3-96704-139-2

For more information, and to order books, please visit www.gestalten.com

Bibliographic information published by the Deutsche Nationalbibliothek. The Deutsche Nationalbibliothek lists this publication in the Deutsche Nationalbibliografie; detailed bibliographic data is available online at www.dnb.de

None of the content in this book was published in exchange for payment by commercial parties or designers; gestalten selected all included work based solely on its artistic merit.

This book was printed on paper certified according to the standards of the FSC®.